INDIA REVEALS HERSELF

INDIA REVEALS HERSELF

BASIL JOSEPH MATHEWS

GYAN

Published by

GYAN

Gyan Publishing House
5, Ansari Road
Daryaganj, New Delhi-110002
Phone: 011-47034999, 9811692060
E-mail: books@gyanbooks.com

Distribution Network
gyanbooks.com
India, USA, Canada, UK, Australia

ISBN: 978-93-7014-821-5 (PB)

First Published, 1937

2nd Impression 2025

Printed at: Gyan Press, Delhi.

INDIA REVEALS HERSELF
Author: BASIL JOSEPH MATHEWS

INDIA REVEALS HERSELF

INDIA REVEALS HERSELF

By BASIL MATHEWS

AUTHOR OF *The Clash of Colour*, *Shaping the Future*, ETC.

With the collaboration of

WINIFRED WILSON

OXFORD UNIVERSITY PRESS

LONDON : HUMPHREY MILFORD

1937

Preface

By its very nature, any claim of this book to present the real trend of life in India to-day depends upon the multitude of direct, intimate talks that I have enjoyed with men and women, young and old, Indian and European, singly and in group discussion, in every walk of life and of many faiths and political attitudes. To reproduce such talks may seem to the reader to savour either of indiscretion or impertinence. In all cases, however, the folk knew that I had in view writing about India. To that end I took extensive notes during the conversations.

If, after exercising every care, it is found that I have unwittingly and unwillingly misrepresented any opinion or idea presented to me, I shall be distressed and penitent. I have every hope, however, that no such blunder has been made.

I owe a debt of gratitude to those in England and in India who gave me introductions in such friendly and general terms as to open doors into the life of men and women who were thus made willing, in turn, to reveal to me many significant insights into the Indian drama whose plot is to-day moving toward a tense crisis. To name all those who have thus given priceless help would make too long a list; to select from them would be impossible where all had such value. Behind them are the friends and colleagues in Britain, Geneva, and America from whose knowledge I have for a quarter of a century been gradually getting a clearer perspective of the changing Indian scene. The debt is equally great to the authors and editors of the books by Indians and

Europeans that have continually enriched my understanding of India ever since thirty years ago lively interest in the land and its people was aroused by S. K. Datta's *The Desire of India*.

One outstanding debt of gratitude must be acknowledged. Miss Winifred Wilson sailed to India and about half-way through my tour joined forces in the happy task of exploring the life of India and of discovering the ferments at work there. On the voyage home to England in a leisurely boat she has collaborated continuously with me in the intensive work of preparing this volume, and bringing to it material from her own independent contacts in India. This colleagueship in assembling, selecting, and arranging the material, and in working out at every stage the line of its presentation has alone made the production of the book possible. The constant discussion of impressions and of points of view has checked hasty judgements and made for more mature and balanced convictions. It is also of priceless value to be able to leave the manuscript in Miss Wilson's hands in England to see through the press, in view of the fact that within a few days of reaching home, I have to hasten to America. There further thanks are due to the authorities of Boston University and Andover-Newton Theological School for their readiness to agree to my stay in India being lengthened in spite of its cutting into my usual term of professorial lectures in America. To Mr. F. H. Brown also I am deeply indebted for reading the book in manuscript and for putting his intimate knowledge of Indian life and affairs at my disposal.

THE ATHENAEUM, LONDON BASIL MATHEWS

February 1937

Contents

AUTHOR'S PREFACE . . . v

I. DISCOVERING INDIA . . . 1

II. LIGHTNING FROM THE NORTH . . 13

III. THE STRATEGIC PEASANT . . . 27

IV. 'EXCRESCENCE' OR 'HERO' . . . 35

V. RENAISSANCE UNDER ALIEN RULE . . 50

VI. CITY OF PILGRIMS 62

VII. THE BENGAL CAULDRON . . . 75

VIII. GATEWAY OF EAST AND WEST . . 90

IX. SEATS OF THE MIGHTY . . . 109

X. THE FACE OF MOTHER INDIA . . 122

XI. INDIA OF THE PRINCES . . . 142

XII. THE BEAUTY OF AJANTA . . . 153

XIII. WHITHER? 163

INDEX 190

CHAPTER I

Discovering India

INCESSANT lightning threw the Western Ghats into indigo silhouette as the *Maloja* drove through the night southward over the Indian Ocean. A monsoon storm was breaking on the hills of Travancore. I could imagine the peasant farmer, as the rain thrashed down on his palm-leaf thatch, rejoicing at the waters for his paddy-fields. Within a few hours I should be passing by the men wading in those fields; I should be able to see the toddy-men climb the palm-trees and watch their brothers punting their craft up the backwaters. As I leant on the taffrail of the ship a strange excitement of questioning grew. For over twenty-five years I had been longing to discover India for myself; preparing to understand her; trying to become equipped to attempt even to interpret her. Now at long last the day had come. It took a man's breath away. For three months I had nothing in the world to do but to concentrate during every waking hour of the day on the discovery of India. I was to face the adventure when India was on the verge of the greatest political experiment that the world has ever seen: the launching of a new constitution on which hangs the relationship of a sixth of the human race with the British Commonwealth of Nations. I was to explore India when the secular ferments of nationalism and socialism are beginning to work their transformation in even the seven hundred thousand villages of India; when every phase of Indian life from the wider family unit to the structure of caste is suffering change; and when even the seventy million outcastes are beginning to threaten either to hammer their way into the temples or to turn their backs upon Hinduism for ever.

I wanted to discover India—the real India—and, while sitting at the feet of the students and seers who have interpreted India to us, to discover India for myself—not the India of yesterday but of to-day—and still more to appraise, not the surface ripples or the local eddies, but those strong steady currents and trends that will flow on to shape the India of to-morrow.

What chance, I asked myself, looking eastward across the waters to the thunderstorm breaking over India, what chance had I of achieving this? How could I get any realistic perception of the Indian scene in so short a time over so vast an area? How could any lucid true way be traced through the confused forest of issues, whose roots go down often into pre-history, and whose branches are nevertheless buffeted by the winds of twentieth-century world forces?

Little enough chance, I realized. Some favours, however, fortune had offered me to this end. At every stage of the projected travel into all parts of India from Trivandrum and Madura in the far south to Delhi and Lahore in the north-west, and from Bengal in the east to Bombay in the west, I had introductions to men and women in whose hands were the keys of understanding to every side of Indian life. Thus the door was open into the real confidence of liberals and of devotees of the old ways; of Dewans of Indian States and of Governors of British provinces; of rebels and revolutionaries; of civil servants and orators, editors and poets, judges and condemned prisoners; of nationalists, imperialists, and communists; of pioneers of women's progress and advocates of purdah; of men and women, both Indian and European, who are giving a life's service to education, to fighting disease, to rural reconstruction and to engineering; of economists and philosophers, mystics, theologians, and traders; of students, professors, and college principals; of Muslims and Hindus, Parsis and Buddhists, Sikhs, Christians, and hearty young pagan atheists.

Nor, as the event proved, was I at the mercy of that subtle deceiver, the courtesy that tells the listening stranger what it is thought he wishes to hear rather than the truth. For I practised everywhere the method of getting men of differing views to discuss with one another while I 'listened-in', often forgotten by them in the zest of argument. I had no thesis to prove; no axe to grind; no one side of Indian life on which to concentrate; no organization to serve.

Perhaps the crowning mercy in the equipment for the discovery of India is that, ever since it was my good fortune, as an embryo student of modern history and political philosophy at Oxford, to be put under the tutorial direction of Ernest Barker, I had incessantly tried to develop the mental and emotional discipline of research that he helped me to practise there, with a view to an intimate just appraisal of the life of peoples in the world of to-day against the perspective of the past. And everywhere, whether in London, Geneva, or Boston, the friendship, at times the close colleagueship, of Indians like K. T. Paul and S. K. Datta, and of lifelong students of India like Sir Valentine Chirol and J. N. Farquhar, has been a priceless gift.

Indeed, when I came to look at it, my real problem

was to be prepared to let India reveal herself. This is not simply a question of trying to empty oneself of pride and prejudice, but of cultivating positive imaginative sympathy; not the cold objective detachment of the impartial observer, but a blend of scientific analysis with intuition—the union of historical perspective with psychological insight. No one can reveal himself to you unless you are his friend; and this is so with peoples as well as with individuals.

The story of many of those challenging contacts is told in this book; and of the judgements to which they have led me. Even the picture of India, however, is an education as you move on for thousands and thousands of miles, by train and car, motor-bus and bullock-bandy, and on foot. The multitudinous villages, the endless patchwork of fields, the human procession—men, women, and children—bearing on their heads the harvest of the fields or the water of their wells; the dust of the roads rising from the feet of bullocks trailing the crops of the village to the town-market—all add to the 'endless going on of life' which is India.

From the train you look out on that moving panorama. In the south are wide rivers and mountains and the vivid green of rice-fields, where the women stand ankle-deep in mud transplanting the young seedlings. A wonderfully elaborate system of channels made by hand in the damp earth carries water to these paddy-fields. All the growing things are beautiful: the millions of palm-trees, plantations of bananas, the graceful little tapioca trees, mangoes, and cashew-nut trees. Travelling northward you come into the region of bare sun-baked plains, the villages surrounded by high walls of dried mud. From the train, too, you see the procession of bullock wagons slowly creaking along the dusty roads, north and south. On the banks of rivers or of village tanks men and women are washing their garments in the muddy water, beating them on stones to remove the dirt. A small naked brown boy drives the water-buffaloes before him into the stream. Gloomy slate-grey beasts, they wallow in water or mud, often only their horns and the sharp ridges of their backs visible. Across the bare brown fields moves a file of women, walking gracefully upright in spite of the heavy burdens on their heads, their saris or full swinging skirts of crimson or brick, purple, green or blue, a lovely symphony of colour.

The competition for the water-tap, if you watch it closely enough when the morning train stops at a station like Itarsi, gives you a moving film of half the story of India. The very fact that all through the north stations advertise 'Hindu water' and 'Mohammedan water', running from the same source but out of different taps, is a symbol.

A plump Brahmin of some forty years, his smooth sleek body stripped to the waist, with only the sacred thread over his shoulder and a cotton slip round his hips, squats in the concrete cistern while the tap, turned on full, swishes water down his back. His wife, her hands dripping, stands behind her lord, waiting her chance to cleanse fingers, lips, mouth, and teeth. No sooner have they finished than three men are at the tap. A youth in *khaddar* and the Gandhi cap stands in the cistern with his *dhoti* tucked between his knees. His enthusiastic tooth-cleaning and gargling deserve a film reproduction for the hygienic stimulation of the English elementary schoolboy. A less agile senior squats on the concrete wall of the cistern and swishes water over his face and feet, while a young Punjabi, on the other wall, enjoys the same refreshment. The older man then seizes his small brass jar and holds it under the tap. Before the train starts they are all back in the coaches; hands and feet, mouth and face ceremonially as well as physically cleansed all ready for the morning meal.

This meanwhile has been bought. Youths, shouting their wares, go up and down the platform bearing under their arms light wicker-work stands woven of cane, like two cones with the points together; and carrying on their heads baskets and trays or fly-proof meat-safes of wood and metal-gauze, some round, some oblong. Oranges and plantains, chapatties—the thin round crisp biscuit-bread of India—curry and rice, pass to and fro under the watchful eyes and appreciative noses of the passengers. An upward jerk of the fingers, the hand held palm upward, is the 'come-hither' gesture of India—and it brings the eager merchant to the carriage window where he places his wicker-work stand upright on the platform and his box or tray of wares on top of it.

It is a women's compartment. This we know, not simply because it is packed with women and children, Hindu and Muslim, having the time of their lives watching the great world go by and exchanging joyful and malicious banter and remarks upon the oddities of the rest of us, but because on the outside of the coach by the door is a coloured glass picture of a woman in a sari. This picture is lighted from within at night. The sign reminds us that of the hundred million women travelling in India each year, only a fractionally small percentage can read in any language; while those who can read know, generally speaking, only one of the languages. Quickly a woman makes her purchase, for the station master's assistant is beating with a hammer the hanging length of railway-line that passes for a bell in all the railway stations of India—and, as I was to discover, even in village churches. And her young son is eager to make his white teeth meet through the fresh plantains that she buys.

The man squatting on the roof of the coach filling its lavatory water-tank through a hose-pipe scrambles down to the ground. The newsboys with the Tamil, Telugu, Hindu, or Bengali vernacular newspapers as well as the *Statesman*, the *Hindu*, or the *Madras Mail*, take a last flying run along the platform to incite if only one more passenger to learn the news of the world and part with some pice. The youth who seemed at every railway station in India to regard it as his life-mission to make me buy a terrifying jack-knife with at least fifteen blades—all open and flashing in the sunlight—turns away 'more in sorrow than in anger', baffled for the sixtieth time.

To sit in a third-class railway coach is to realize how it comes about that, in the eight decades since the first railway train ran along its few hundred miles of line in India and the startled world heard that fifty Parsi ladies had risked their lives in its coaches, the railway has constantly and increasingly been at work as a force for change in the life of India. The jostling of castes and creeds in the train, the coming together of men from every province and principality, has been a strong factor both in opening fissures in the four-square citadel of the caste system and in weaving the fabric of an all-India mentality.

Day and night across the loom of India's immense railway system the trains pass like shuttles to and fro and the people in them are in incessant talk. I say day and night, for the darkness brings no cessation. However deeply the misguided Indian merchants and British or American sahibs may sleep in their first- or second-class coaches, India itself, the real India that takes some six hundred million third-class railway tickets a year, is not so stupid as to waste the precious drama-filled hours of the night in slumber. The Punjabi farmer—his legs tucked up under him—seated between the Marathi money-lender and the Afghan horse-dealer and face to face with the young journalist from Madras and the commercial traveller in hurricane lamps who dwells everywhere, talks and listens all night. For at his journey's end he knows he will have stories with which to make both the eyes and ears of every man in his village open with astonishment for months.

The whips of conversation in the men's coach, however, are without sting compared with the scorpions of the women's compartment. Imagine the thrill when you, as a Hindu or Muslim wife of a small shopkeeper or a village blacksmith, have been cooped up in the tiny courtyard of your home and for years have rarely talked with any one beyond the group around the village well or the market stall, find yourself let loose in a crowded coach of other women similarly released. Here is no local back-biter to tell on you, and no superior man to put bridle and bit on your speech. The life-story of every woman in the coach is overhauled; she is cross-questioned—and would feel injured if it were not so—as to her parents, husband, and children.

Even the European woman who ventures into a women's third-class coach has to submit to the fire of questions and to listen to a frank but good-natured discussion of her appearance, clothes, and peculiarities. The train is the true circulating library of India's illiterate womanhood; a whole shelf-ful of short stories straight from life, palpitating, unexpurgated, humorous, indignant, scathing, pathetic; enough to tax the pen of a Balzac in a lifetime's effort to reproduce *La Comédie Indienne.*

Yet even to the sahib who slumbers, whether uneasily or easily, through the hot dusty night in his second-class compartment, an Indian journey is an education. This book could be filled with the record of talks in the train. A man in a fez is seated in the corner reading *Daily Light for Daily Needs.* I go to lunch and come back; he is still meditating on it as it lies open on his knee. We talk. He is a Professor of Economics in a Muslim college in one of the Indian States. I find that he never travels without that well-thumbed little anthology.

'I do not understand,' he tells me, 'how any man goes on living and facing the problems of his life unless he can get some daily light and meditates on it.' If, however, in a work of fiction the writer introduced a Muhammadan professor, who had studied economics under a rationalist like H. A. L. Fisher, reading a devotional product of British Victorian evangelicalism in an Indian train, he would be derided for letting an inebriated imagination run riot. There was, again, the cynical Tamil retired civil servant who reads English current biography, travel, politics, and science incessantly, and who scorns the new vernacular literature in the Indian languages as a pathetic sterile mule born of an unnatural union of imitative provincial patriotism with western modernism—the back number trying to take the forward look.

My thought runs back also to the young Muslim couple encountered in a train. The wife, coquettish, obviously charming, was covered from head to foot in a *bourkah*—not the white shroud-like garment of the strict Muslim—but deep purple silk, with thick gold lattice work over the face, through which her lustrous dark eyes glinted. Demurely she sat in her corner, shrouded, mysterious, gazing at the western woman with her workaday cotton frock and short hair, who was discussing some problem with me. 'If that is equality,' you could imagine her thinking, 'then I don't want it!' Through the veil she turned her eyes on the young husband at her side. He caught her face in his hands, turned her gaze towards himself, swinging aside the veil so that he could look into her eyes. He bent over her with kisses and murmured endearments. Later, when she sat silent again in her corner, he told us that he was a broadcast announcer, a western-educated man living by one of the latest scientific discoveries of the West. 'I want my wife to come out of purdah,' he said, a little apologetically, 'but she won't.' Did he really wish it, I wondered. Was she perhaps wise to sustain the subtle flattery of beauty shown to him alone?

How I longed to extend the journey with the Indian school-inspector whose whole life is spent in trying to stimulate under-paid half-trained teachers in schools and villages and little towns to educate their pupils and not do sporadic cramming for purgatorial examinations! There was also the man who travels all the time selling oil and encouraging the sale of those little power-engines that are beginning to pump the village tanks for irrigation, to thresh the rice harvest and grind the rye. The sheer story of his commercial travel shed another side-light on the slow penetration of rural India by the transforming mechanisms of the West. How friendly, how deliciously inquisitive, how beautifully opinionated, how pathetically eager for the opening of a window on the life of other lands and peoples are the men of India!

Startled at seeing a motor-bus bounding along the roads of Travancore boldly labelled the *Mahatma*, I wondered what Mr. Gandhi would have thought of that title for this projectile of the 'Satanic' western mechanistic civilization. For to-day the bus is outstripping the train as a carrier of ferment into the peasant life of India. As the millions of Indian rats carry plague, so the thousands upon thousands of buses, always crammed with passengers, and carrying them from the village to the city and back, carry the virus of modernism. The Indian bus must not be thought of in terms of the cushioned, balloon-tyred limousine of Britain or America. It is often an elevated toast-rack of wooden seats on a Ford commercial chassis, with a crude 'purdah' section in front whose torn curtains flap in the breeze.

In my first week in India I sat in a large Tinnevelly village talking with the pastor of a great church that has just celebrated its centenary; and asking him what new trends he sees in the life of the younger generation. His story of change all comes back to the motor-bus. 'The young people,' he said, 'go in the bus to the town;

they go to the cinemas and see the films that shake them from the ways of their fathers. They become restless and independent; they have lost something and have found nothing to replace it.' Even in an area like Erode in the Madras Presidency, relatively remote from the infection that great cities bring, I found that the youths in many villages reckon even out of their tiny income to run by bus to Erode once a week to see the pictures. These boys can be seen, I was told, framing their behaviour on their favourite film hero as faithfully as their western sisters emulate the coiffure of a Greta Garbo or of a Katherine Hepburn.

. . . .

The wheels of the train and the bus, the loaded bullock wagon, and the trotting tonga carried much of India before me. It was partly through the 'whirling of wheels', as Ezekiel puts it, that India revealed herself to me, as I tried to penetrate to the ambitions and the fears, the loves and hates, the conflict of loyalties, and the adventures toward new life beneath that entrancing many-coloured cavalcade.

CHAPTER II

Lightning from the North

As I drove past the gaily dressed crowds going in and out of the Lahore Zoo on my way to call on Begum Shah Nawaz, I could not help speculating on this leader of Islamic womanhood to whom Sir Abdul Qadir of London had given me an introduction. I knew that her father had been one of the first Muslims in all India to bring his women-folk out of purdah. The appointment to have tea with her was, I was aware, a breathing spell in a hectic political campaign under the new constitution granted to India in which she was a candidate for election to represent the Unionist party. My imagination framed a picture of a rather hurried earnest interview sandwiched between committees and letters dictated to private secretaries. How different was the reality! In her beautiful drawing-room, by the fireplace in which leaping flames kept at bay the frost in the Christmas air, stood a lady in an exquisite sari edged with gold, its folds framing an oval face, on whose calm clear-cut contour and thoughtful yet humorous eyes her strenuous life had carved no single line. Into the room there began to float one after the other happy lively young folk—two of her daughters with some of their friends, the wife of a British officer, the young proprietor and editor of the one monthly magazine in the Punjab which gives a cultural lead to India's north, and a lively, beloved, adopted uncle whose witty cynicisms made him always the centre of a laughing group. The Begum's husband sent his regrets that doctor's orders kept him from facing the strain of social life.

Nowhere in any western drawing-room could such a symphony of exquisite colour and line and movement be found. I watched across the heads of the editor and the uncle, who were talking to me, the young folk moving to and fro, each sari a poem of light and shade as the firelight played about it and gleamed in the finely wrought silver and gold ear-rings and brooches. Yet only a day or two earlier Begum Shah Nawaz was on the platform at a political meeting when chairs were hurled about in fury as she was speaking. At another meeting for women only, women concealed in bourkahs stood up and shook their fists under her nose because she, a Muslim woman, wore no veil and thus betrayed the faith.

Would I like to see *Romeo and Juliet* with Norma Shearer and John Barrymore? There was just time to change and get to the theatre, where I found that our hostess had taken fifteen seats. Fascinating though the film was, it was still more thrilling to trace the swift reactions of a preponderantly Indian house to the torrent of Mercutio's sophisticated wit, to the crescendo of intolerable tragedy, and, above all, to the white flame of Romeo's and Juliet's romantic love. There flashed into my mind sentences from C. S. Lewis's new book, *The Allegory of Love*, which I had read on the way out to India:

'French poets, in the eleventh century, discovered or invented, or were the first to express, that romantic species of passion which English poets were still writing about in the nineteenth. They effected a change which has left no corner of our ethics, our imagination, or our daily life untouched, and they erected impassable barriers between us and the classical past or the oriental present.'

Even as I had read those words about the chasm between the contemporary West and East created by the conception of romantic love, my mind had questioned it. But discussion with Indian friends on the ship and with numbers in centre after centre in India had revealed the element of truth in it in a land where, under the joint family system, the husband and wife were chosen for each other. No thought of love enters there. The girl marries not so much a husband but into the family. Her function is to extend it. Yet it was easy to see that even under that system romantic love would grow up, as all India's classical literature shows. As a young Indian laughingly put it to me, 'In the West you fall in love and then marry, in the East we marry and then fall in love.' Again I discovered, of course, that the joint system is being severely shaken. Men and women to an increasing though still infinitesimal degree are beginning to choose their mates. Reflection on *Romeo and Juliet* revealed the exciting fact that here in Shakespeare's play was the very conflict of which I have just spoken in India—the fight of the individualism of romantic love, with one woman and one man moving towards each other, against the embattled resistance of the Montagues and Capulets of Asia. A tragic little cutting from an Indian daily paper concentrates a blinding spotlight on a single example of the struggle that I am convinced has its example in any considerable city in India:

'A suicide pact between a Hindu girl and her lover has come to light following the deaths of the youth and the girl, both by arsenic poisoning. According to a statement alleged to have been made by the girl just before her death, she was married recently against her wishes to another youth, but managed to return to Lahore from her husband's house and continued her friendship with her lover. She was to have been sent back to her husband's house, and in view of the impending separation she and her lover decided to die rather than be separated.'

In thousands and thousands of cinemas in India today, from Darjeeling to Trivandrum, from Bombay to Calcutta, Indian as well as western films are flickering the story of romantic love before the eyes of India's young people. And not only in cities but; as we shall see later, in country towns where village youths by the hundred thousand spend a regular weekly two annas (about 2*d.*) on what has become to them a necessary escape from the stark monotony of their lives.

One of India's innumerable contrasts broke on me in going to tea the next day at the home of Miss K. B. Feroze-ud-Din, who performs what I would have thought to be the incredible feat of combining strict purdah, including, of course, the wearing of the all-enveloping bourkah, with holding the office of Inspector of Education of a very large area of the Punjab, the Presidency of the Graduate Women's Association of Punjab University, and the Presidency of the All-India Women's Muslim Conference, as well as achieving the reputation of being one of the most convincing women speakers in India. Her drawing-room mantelpiece was simply covered with what looked like Christmas cards, though it seemed obvious that in the house of a thoroughly orthodox Muslim they could not be. Examination showed that they were the exact equivalent of our Christmas cards but were linked up with the Muslim feast at the end of the Fast of Ramazan. On card after card that I took up I saw 'With sincere greetings for a merry Id', sometimes in odd comradeship with a picture of an English thatched cottage. Toward the end of my talk with her brother over tea Miss Feroze-ud-Din came into the drawing-room, completely concealed in her bourkah. Her entire approach to education and to social reform, as well as to women's future in both these regions, is governed by the conviction that religion must control the whole life of man, and she put forward a very vigorous if not completely convincing argument on the essential freedom of the life of woman under Muhammad's own teaching. In respect of education she recalled that the first message the Prophet received from Allah was to read and that this was repeated three times; while she interprets the teaching that woman's place is in the home not as meaning the four walls of the house but the whole social environment and city which is the natural sphere of the home.

As a Muslim educationist Miss Feroze-ud-Din is naturally a convinced opponent of co-education; but her whole energy is thrown into raising the level of popular education in India, especially among village people. Where resolutions are passed at her meetings, she told me, they are always resolutions not to ask for things but to do them. Miss Feroze-ud-Din is a scholar in five or six languages and a busy writer of articles. It seems strange that with such an outlook and activity she should sustain the obviously cramping restrictions of purdah, which means that her face must never be seen by any man outside the inner circle of her own family. She has a utilitarian defence for this, in that if she did not wear the bourkah she would, as an education officer, spend a good deal of time answering the questions and dealing with the problems of all and sundry. As it is, she can concentrate upon the very urgent and clamant problems of women, and freed from distractions she is able to get on with her study and her writing.

To find myself within a few hours talking to the husband of a Muslim woman flying 'ace' was still another of those swift and dramatic transitions which any visitor who gets below the surface of Indian life must be prepared to enjoy. Mr. S. Nitiaz Ali Taj is the proprietor and editor of a girls' and women's weekly and monthly, the title of which would be called in English *The Culture of Women.* His heroic father and mother started this periodical in 1898. I say heroic because when the father floated the paper and the mother edited it, violent attacks were made upon them both. Some people even took the loathsome step of floating temporarily another paper for women edited by a well-known prostitute and then published the news that there were two weekly papers for women, one edited by Mr. Ali Taj's mother, the other by a prostitute. The father sent copies of the paper to get it known to Muslim men on the Civil List, that is in the Indian Civil Service, and almost every one sent his copy back, refusing to let the ladies of his harem see it. Posters were plastered on the walls against the editor. For five years this incessant fight went on till the tide turned. After ten years of this editing the mother died and the present editor's sister took it on. To-day it is a prosperous weekly and monthly, with a growing circulation. The proprietor suggested that his wife, who, as I have said, is the first Muslim woman air pilot in the world, might edit the paper. She declined to do so unless she had an absolutely free hand, without any interference from her husband. This he felt to be impossible because, as he puts it, he knows the temperament of practically every subscriber and how easy it would be to shatter circulation. She retorts: 'Yes, you see all these points from the standpoint of a man, but women can discuss these things more freely with one another.' She is, her husband says, a good imaginative writer, producing short stories and prose poems. The paper, which is published in Urdu and is illustrated, covers a very wide range of subjects. The number through which I went with the proprietor had in it an article on the vote, a short story of Galsworthy, foreign news from all over the world of things interesting to women, articles on teaching little things to children, embroidery, colds and coughs, the revolt in Spain, animals that emit light, the pygmies of Congo, a one-act play, children's ribbon pictures, and so on. The Department of Public Instruction of the Punjab buys a considerable number every month for free distribution in schools for Muslim children.

I passed from one to another of these Muslim moderns through old Lahore. I went out of the broad boulevard swept by breezes and open to the full blaze of the sun into narrow bazaars where, if a laden donkey comes trotting along, the pedestrian steps aside into the coppersmith's booth to let him pass. You must look up to see where the sun catches the Rembrandt-brown carven shutters of overhanging balconies. The exuberant craftsmanship of woodcarvers in Lahore was lavished on such enchanting lattices as those when Elizabeth ruled England. The monsoons of centuries have thrashed across these roofs and scoured the richly ornamented balustrades from which twenty generations have looked down on the endless movement of men and beasts. I watched the smith tinning the interior of his copper cooking vessels. Round his tiny charcoal fire men passed into the mosque. The loveliness of its patterned tiles makes a catch in the breath, for they give back a delicate intensity of turquoise and cypress-green, buttercup yellow and rose, the secret of which is buried for ever with those artist craftsmen. The white-bearded, turbanned silk merchant broods over his accounts and unfolds dream fabrics whose play of light and shade conjures reluctant rupees from the deepest pouch. The vendor of sweetmeats sells to a veiled woman, while the sandal-maker and saddler chatters with a horse-merchant; and all move aside as the treble and tenor of swinging bells mark the passing of a caravan of camels from Peshawar.

Under the bazaar balconies the merchants sit each in his little booth. In those shadowy alleys away to the left live, they say, many thousands of the courtesans for whom Lahore is noted. The Brahmin priest rolls on his way and the sweeper cringes by the open drain at the side. The Muslim horse-dealer steps briskly toward the mosque not to be late for his sunset prayer. In boy after keen-eyed mischievous boy I can see Kim in the bazaars of Lahore. Here more than anywhere in the world—far more than in the motor-distracted streets of Oxford—I hear the whisper of 'the last enchantments of the Middle Ages'.

As our steps climb a slope near the North Gate we wonder why this hill should rise here on this plain. It is, in fact, not a natural hill. It is made up of the debris of eleven cities, the ruin wrought by conqueror after conqueror, storming down the Khyber Pass and breaking the rulers softened by their rich court life. So before ever William the Conqueror took Britain, Ghazni the

Idol Smasher, raging into Lahore, smashed the rule of the Bahmani Kings from Kabul. For centuries wave after wave from the virile north came through breaches they made in the northern walls. Even the imperial Mogul despots—Akbar, Shah Jehan, and Aurungzeb—had their struggles to protect their court within these walls till at last the Persians broke their way in, to be driven out in turn by the Afghans. And their throne was at last seized by the Sikhs who, under Ranjit Singh, restored the city's splendour until Britain took hold—and another Ranjit Singh, in no way related to 'the Lion of the Punjab', became the idol of every British schoolboy.

Standing by that gate of the North, brooding over the marvels that must lie buried in that debris, we can almost see the cavalcade of the centuries come sweeping through on elephant, camel, and horse. Within five minutes I am away from it all in a smart restaurant, all cubes and chromium plate, the guest of a young Muslim married couple, the sound of whose gay chatter fails to compete with the unbridled jazz of a too-enthusiastic saxophone devotee.

An hour or two later I had the lively shock of meeting an Indian Bernard Shaw in a Muslim drawing-room. In order to discover the background of the most powerful poet, Sir Mohammed Iqbal, who has done creative work in northern India within a hundred years, I sat down to talk with a brilliant middle-aged essayist retired into freedom from the Indian Civil Service. In the course of that approach provocative and stimulating epigrams swept to the surface like bubbles in champagne. These sparkling epigrams and challenging paradoxes of Mr. Aziz, scattered as they seemed, all bubbled up from the central gift of Iqbal's poetry, which has made him such a revolutionary force. Some three to four decades ago Iqbal came as a young man into a world where the Persian poet Hali was chanting passionate laments for the fallen greatness of Islam. Hali brought a tremendous awakening to the glory of the past and intense grief at the degradation of the Muslim world. Musliins were holding meetings, especially in northern India and Persia, simply to read his poetry and feel the nostalgia of Islam's glory. Suddenly, at the end of the nineteenth century, Iqbal broke in on the scene, crying, 'Arise, awake, there is going to be no other resurrection if you do not awaken now.' When Iqbal came back as a student from Heidelberg and Munich, Nietzsche had burnt into the Muslim poet's consciousness with his will to power and his superman. Iqbal found deep in the roots of being a common attitude between Muhammad and Nietzsche—the assertion of the manly view, the affirmation of struggle, the refusal of the tiger to accept the sheep's invitation to be a lamb. 'Be a diamond and not a dewdrop', cried Iqbal. He recited his poems as the old troubadours had. Aziz, who as a youngster heard the poems recited by Iqbal, said to me in his cynical way—'Even when I knew it was all humbug I just wept when I heard him'.

Swiftly the tide began to turn. Young Islam forsook misery and lamentation for the eloquence of affirmation. Iqbal attacked mysticism in religion, declaring 'that the very glance of a man of true faith is enough to change the world'. He called to Muslims to let life spring out and be released and he stirred men to a new élan. This led Aziz to one of his more cruel paradoxes. 'Nietzsche and Muhammad', he said, 'are both epileptic philosophers. Nietzsche himself is at his best in his outbursts. He was a precursor of the paragraphist. The same', he went on, 'is true of the fiery eloquence of the Koran; there are passages in the Koran that leave you stunned.' A biting attack on Mahatma Gandhi came straight out of this assertion of a virile grip of reality. 'Gandhi', said Mr. Aziz, 'is India's great crime. We can never expiate that. It seems inconceivable that in the twentieth century such a man, raised to such a point of fame, should still be harking back. He is clamouring for temple entry just when India's great need is to be led away from the temples. This world has not yet begun', Aziz went on. 'This bad dream we are in will pass away and then all things will begin. The essence of moral progress', he added, 'is that man continues to change his former old habits for new bad ones. In an age when even light does not go straight, how can we? We have inherited not knowledge but the mistakes of two thousand years.' And as I listened I felt that Aziz was at least living up to his own desire expressed when he said to me, 'All that I ask of God is that neither he nor his people be dull.' One can understand that my friend's Urdu pen-name means 'Wanderer in the Firmament'.

I was now thoroughly prepared to go to meet Sir Mohammed Iqbal himself. I was fortunate in finding him at a time when his recently persistent ill health, which has often made him unable to use his voice, was less troublesome. I found him on a bed pulling occasionally at a hookah which contained some herb to ease his asthma. The hair brushed so that it stood upright and the moustache reminiscent of the ex-Kaiser gave one the feeling that the period of his youth spent in Germany had left a permanent impression on him. The high brow and the full high cheekbones with strong eyebrows over brown eyes, at once humorous and penetrating, gave the instant impression of a restless, masterful, radio-active spirit. On being questioned, however, he denied at once that Nietzsche's influence really touched him in Germany, where he took a degree in 1907–8, after a year or two in England. He confessed that when he was learning German in Heidelberg one student friend used to read aloud *Also Sprach Zarathustra.* He read Nietzsche's books after returning to India, 'and my trend of thought', said Sir Mohammed, 'is different from Nietzsche's. He does not believe in the reality of evil. My own thought rests on the conviction of that reality. Really', he continued, 'Nietzsche was a man of deep religious consciousness, but was misled. If one of the old Muslim religious leaders, trained in the religious psychology of their disciples, had met Nietzsche when he was young he would have discovered the God for whom he was seeking and not remained content with the superman. The wise men of Germany who took no share in love or intoxication had Nietzsche medically treated when he ought to have been spiritually treated. Nietzsche was what we call a *mutsub*—a man absorbed in a single idea, what is in a sense a mad sort of love-frenzy. Woe to the *mutsub* who is born in Europe', he concluded.

If health permits, Sir Mohammed nourishes the ambition of going to Germany to analyse on the spot the records of the treatment given to Nietzsche, in the belief that he will find it to have been misguided at every point. 'Nietzsche saw the light of God but did not know that he saw it. He remained away from it as a fruit is remote from its root. He was a man who knew the way he never found, and so he broke himself from God as well as from himself.'

Iqbal's whole poetry, like his philosophy, in writing about which he has indulged in later years, is rooted in the affirmation of life. This runs, for instance, through the only book of his that is translated into English, *The Secret of the Self*, of which Professor Nicholson's translation cannot, of course, convey the lilt and intoxication of the marvellous Persian original.

The intense centre of Iqbal's philosophy is to be had in the philosophical phrase 'the identity of the ego'. He told me how Professor Spooner argued with him for long to prove the non-identity of the ego. Iqbal retorted, 'I am admitting your argument, but who is the arguer?' 'The world', he went on, 'is visible but stands in need of argument to affirm it—the ego is invisible but needs no argument. You know of its existence by intuition. I am force, I am power, I can do something.'

I asked him whether Kemal Ataturk, in making Turkey forceful and powerful, had not turned his back on Islam as the source of Turkey's weakness. He heartily affirmed that Turkey has turned her back not on Islam but on mysticism, which is the enemy. Buddhistic mysticism has affected Islam. It is the parent of the doctrine of fate, which has ruined the Islamic world. True Islamic mysticism affirms the material world and does not deny it; it says the material is a form of self-realization. We have to conquer the material world and tear it to pieces and not run away from it. Muhammad in that sense was a great mystic. You do not destroy the material; you conquer its powers as modern science is doing.

I came away glowing with admiration for the penetration, the brilliance, and the warmth of feeling that make Sir Mohammed Iqbal's work so creative. I could not help feeling, however, that when he talked of Islam in relation to Turkey or to modern philosophy, there was some danger of his being like a conjuror who pulls out of a hat the rabbits he has himself put in; and that of him, as well as of the brilliant essayist, The Wanderer in the Firmament, it might be true to say that if a man can utter a half-truth as a dogmatism it is more effective than the whole truth.

CHAPTER III

The Strategic Peasant

'THE doctrine of transmigration', growled Sam Higginbottom, as we stumped round his farm near the banks of the sacred Jumna, 'is the greatest economic enemy of India.' I raised my eyebrows at this astonishing statement from a man whose mind seemed concentrated on cows rather than on the higher metaphysics. And I was right; his mind was still concentrated on cows. 'In India', he went on to say, 'there are over sixty cattle to every hundred humans, and well over ninety per cent of them are a dead economic loss. The cows do not produce even enough milk, manure, or offspring to pay for their own board.'

As I had watched the cattle wandering round the streets of almost every city from Calcutta to Madura, undergrown, scraggy, parasites, I had felt how wasteful they were. But now that I realized through Higginbottom's eyes that they ran into hundreds of millions, eating up food that the children of India need and not paying for their board in milk, new light came on the murderous nature of a doctrine of transmigration that makes the sacred cow starve the human. But this is only the beginning of the picture. The rat, who is the incarnation of a popular god, may not be slain. Yet the rat is not only a carrier of vermin which disseminate plague, but it is scientifically credited now with the destruction of ten per cent of the annual crop of India's grain. Something like ten million tons of grain per year are destroyed by the rat. The monkey, again, is sacred because of the monkey-god, Hanuman, and for that reason there are numerous villages throughout India where no fruit or vegetables can be found because of the toll taken by monkeys. The wild pig is not killed because of the sacredness of life—nor is the wild deer. Yet there are enormous herds of deer and droves of wild pigs which raid the crops of the villager. In uncounted villages the peasant dare grow only those crops which the wild pig refuses to eat. So Sam Higginbottom goes straight back to the beginning of Genesis for the basis of a new economic life for India—man shall 'have dominion over every living thing that moveth on the earth'. To him, in his own words, 'the Indian people are lovely, but they are the victims of a system of ideas that gives no plan or programme for triumphant life.'

He showed me cows whose great-grandmothers produced barely twelve hundred pounds of milk in three hundred days, but who were themselves producing three thousand pounds. In twenty years he has increased the yield of wool from sheep from one pound to five pounds —wool of so long a staple and so soft that the mills pay thirty-five rupees for eighty-two pounds of it as against sixteen rupees for the same amount from an ordinary Indian sheep.

Travelling through the length and breadth of India I found, especially following Lord Linlithgow's lead, that all India is cow-conscious. The provision of stud bulls has become almost fashionable; rural reconstruction is the rage. Under the new constitution the peasant, because of his vote, has become important, so all the world is seeking his favour. Some are utterly sincere and wish him good, some are just fishermen angling for votes and baiting their hook with promises as politicians do in every country. The chasm that divides the copyist from the creative artist lies between these last and such a man as Higginbottom. Half English, half Welsh, he came to India a third of a century ago. Having gathered all the biology that an American university could give him he put it at the feet of the Indian peasant for the love of a Master whom village people heard gladly nearly two thousand years ago.

Walking down the tortuous lanes between mud huts we saw a picture of untouched peasant life that would be true of hundreds of thousands of other villages. A man sat on the earth patiently chopping a thick-stemmed crop into food for his cow, a scraggy animal that stood alongside, her ribs jutting like corrugated iron through her skin. The fodder was infected with a red preventible disease that reduced its nourishing value by over a third. All around lay the cow-dung cakes drying in the sun for fuel, the precious manure of which the fields were starved. On a string bed lay a baby, his face and eyes and naked body swarming with disease-carrying flies from the dung-cakes. The child made no effort to drive away the flies which seemed caked in a solid mass around his eyes. We saw in the making one of the uncounted multitudes of India's blind. A few steps farther on a woman scoured with a cake of cow-dung the vessel in which the family food was cooked. The washing-up place was a dirty puddle in the ground. Scavenging pigs thrust their searching snouts into every nook or cranny for either human or cattle ordure.

If we ask why the villager does not use the dung for the fields, the absence of other fuel in many parts is an answer. But the unmanured field means a poor crop, and the poor crop means emaciated people and cattle.

Their listlessness through under-feeding, malaria, hook-worm, and other diseases paralyses initiative. The almighty shackles of custom cramp all movement. The doctrine of *karma*—the one universal conviction of Indians—shows that what comes to you is the inevitable outcome of earlier acts and there is, therefore, no use in resistance. As the hammer blows of one after another of these obstacles to all improvement beat upon one, admiration grows to wonder at the sheer grit that can keep going through a third of a century to bring more life and abundant into this colossal lethargy. Yet lethargy, from another angle, conveys an utterly wrong impression. From dawn to dark the peasant is at work, the woman at her household tasks, the man in the fields or at his handicraft, sowing third-rate seed in starved soil and breeding tenth-rate cattle to serve undernourished humans, working with time-wasting implements—all this everywhere under the economic despotism of the money-lender and often the blood-sucking of the zemindar's (landlord's) remorseless middle-men.

The only drama I discovered in the life of this village was provided by a Hindu-Muslim quarrel. A Muslim had snatched the wife of a Hindu peasant and hidden her behind the purdah. The Hindu beat the Muslim. To and fro the feud went with beatings and burnings, raids and counter-raids. At last both sides, caught in this vicious endless spiral, appealed to Mr. and Mrs. Higginbottom for arbitration. Their sanctified common sense and humour, added to the authority that their long unselfish service brought, at last healed the wound that neither law nor force could cure.

Among the scraggy beasts in that village we had noted more substantial animals with larger milk-bearing capacity, whose parentage went back to Higginbottom's bulls. Here and there in these villages improvements showed themselves through the use of better seed, the more economic handling of irrigation from the well, the production of larger eggs from chickens whose strain had been improved from Higginbottom's Agricultural Institute near Allahabad. As, however, I went the round of his fields and saw his animals, putting them mentally beside the relatively unchanged village, the feeling deepened that the baffling enigma that has not yet been solved does not lie so much in the region of developing techniques but of gearing them into the daily life of the village.

Moving through the villages of India, peering into the darkness of outcaste hovels, looking into the haggard, famished faces of their inmates and at their emaciated bodies I felt that here was not much sign of 'mystical India'. Millions of Indians are not wondering about their souls, but they are desperately anxious as to where the next meal is coming from. Countless thousands do not know from one year to another how it feels to have their hunger appeased; in times of scarcity they may be reduced to a handful of leaves a day for food. Among the outcastes are rat-eaters who, when they have caught a brood of rats, gather up grain by grain the fragments of green-mouldy rice that the rats have stored and take it home to eat. There are in India at least sixty to seventy millions hanging on the edge of the abyss of starvation. Nevertheless, among the middle castes, who are the great solid foundation of the Indian structure of life, the economic level, though terribly low, is not altogether desperate.

In these more prosperous villages the houses are larger and better constructed; there are probably one or two small shops and a Hindu temple, or a mosque if the inhabitants are Muslims. There is a cheery din from the blacksmith's shed, the whirr of a sewing machine from the mud veranda where the village tailor sits cross-legged with the garments of a bride's trousseau scattered round him; the potter is busy at his wheel making earthenware vessels, and the women return buoyantly from the well. The village streets, however, even in the better villages, are narrow and unpaved and generally full of garbage and filth, with stagnant pools that breed mosquitoes. There is very little sanitation, and epidemics of small-pox and cholera take their toll of the defenceless villagers.

Out in the fields the peasant farmer patiently tills his scanty acres, able to raise sufficient for his needs so long as no calamity overtakes him. But he is so near the margin that divides subsistence from starvation that he lives ever in dread of delayed or scanty rains, of floods, of sickness or death among his meagre cattle and goats, of the expense of a wedding or a funeral in the family.

In areas like Bengal, again, where the villager has come to depend upon single crops for export like jute, millions are smitten into the dust by a world collapse of prices. Over India, also, as a whole, the purchase of agricultural implements from Birmingham and Pittsburg that once were made by the village blacksmith, and the buying of hurricane lanterns in place of the earthenware lamp with its flickering wick, bleeds the village of economic strength that was once a mainstay.

I have here given a fairly sharply focused close-up of the situation which creates India's greatest problem and of one notable experiment toward grappling with it. The hopeful element in the scene lies partly in the multiplicity of adventurous enterprises in all parts of India toward rural reconstruction. Many of these, like Mr. Higginbottom's, are under Christian auspices; others, more recently, work through secular and reformed Hindu agencies. We shall return to some of these later from a different angle. Viewed separately they look sporadic, isolated, and puny compared with the colossal task. Seen, however, against the darkness of earlier lethargy they are gleams of dawn. Viewed also in the light of the fact that the Chairman of the Royal Commission on Agriculture that for the first time surveyed the total problem is now Viceroy of India, an element of coherence and common purpose comes into all this expenditure of energy. It would seem as though even those who are most heavily overborne by the immensity and complexity of the obstacles ahead should take new heart of hope.

As I looked across the Indian scene the conviction grew that a solution of the problem of village life is in process of discovery. In the far south where, under Mr. K. Hatch's indomitable inventive leadership, the Y.M.C.A.'s rural reconstruction centre at Martandum in Travancore is infiltrating new practices slowly but surely over a wide area, from the Punjab with the passionate advocacy of F. L. Brayne to Bengal with Rabindranath Tagore's farm and Sir Daniel Hamilton's model colony, from the Viceroy's inspiring and sustained stimulus to the brilliant experiments in a progressive Indian State like Mysore, there is the sound of a going in the tops of the trees.

The Director of Broadcasting for India, Lionel Fielden, at Delhi, told me how many responses come from villages to broadcast information about better seeds or ways of fending off plant disease. Reliable expert estimates assure us that the soil of India properly handled and with a scientific rotation of crops could support eight times its present population, which is more than the present population of the planet; for we are faced here by a land in which, for the most part, there is no winter and in which, in spite of the absence of rain over much of the year, the governmental development of irrigation, already unique in extent in the whole world, can be enormously expanded.

The element in Indian life that creates its problem is the source of its undying hope—what Lewis, in his *Allegory of Love*, calls 'the ageless fecundity, the endless and multiform going-on of life'.

CHAPTER IV

'Excrescence' or 'Hero'

I CAN count on the fingers of two hands those books which it has been an event in life to read. Of still fewer books is it true to say that having read them I have come to know the very warp and woof of a great personality and the forces shaping the destiny of a great people. Yet as the seven hundred pages of Pandit Jawaharlal Nehru's autobiography rendered their riches as I passed over the Red Sea and the Arabian Sea to his country, this is what happened. As I closed the book I knew that the judgement reported to me as from Lord Halifax was true, that no one can understand contemporary India who has not read that book.

To come face to face with Jawaharlal Nehru and, if it could be, to get leisurely and even intimate talk with him, must be central to the quest of a pilgrim whose search is for the trends and the personalities shaping the new India. Passing through the length and breadth of India and talking with young men and mature leaders, those who frankly denounced him as an 'excrescence' or adored him as the hero of a great renunciation—the man who had gone from his father's mansion to a prison cell and from Harrow and Cambridge to the dust and heat of the Congress struggle—my desire to explore the meaning of Nehru was intensified. Twice I crossed his tracks. The first time was in Madura, in the course of a lightning journey in which he was said to have made one hundred and thirty speeches in a week, counting the occasions when his car was arrested at village after village in the course of a triumphal progress that princes might envy. The shining light in the eyes of students at the American college in Madura revealed the flame of their hero-worship. Yet alongside this I clearly detected a touch of cooling in the temperature of some of those who had heard him speak. His astringent, fearless, blunt laying down of the inner discipline and steady labour needed if success were to be achieved cooled the ardour of the merely emotional hearer, and, on the other hand, like cold water on red-hot metal, toughened the temper of those who took his words to heart. Before I met Nehru it had become clear from contact with those who heard him that this devotee of Marx is to the finger-tips an aristocrat. All that the demagogue is he loathes. If he had been in England during the War, Balfour and not Lloyd George would have been his natural ally. I found the same effect had been created among the students of Calcutta. He denounced noise and disorder in meetings where, I understand, Mahatma Gandhi would have sat cross-legged on the platform until they ceased.

Being anxious at all events to avoid having an interview in the hurly-burly of such whirlwind election campaigns I thought it worth while waiting to see Nehru until he could point out a clear space when he would be in the home that his sister and her husband, Mr. and Mrs. Ranjit Sitaram Pandit, make for him in Allahabad in a small house that his father built alongside the family mansion. It is now Congress headquarters; and even that home can hardly be called a retreat, for pilgrims from all parts come continuously to, so to speak, camp on its verandas in order to get word with him or even a glimpse of his figure as he moves to and fro.

To walk across that veranda and into the house was literally to be at home. His beautiful sister with her husband shared not only prison but authorship in prison with Nehru. They have created a home that blends an almost austere simplicity with calm and comfort, and where the voices of their three young daughters chimed with the discussion of India's future. The eldest daughter from school writes to her mother letters that reveal her caught up, for instance, in intensest interest and detailed knowledge of the Presidential election in the United States or the stages of the Spanish Civil War. We did not meet Nehru's own daughter, to whom he wrote the letters that make his sketch of the history of the world, as she was in England facing entrance into Somerville College, Oxford.

It was a happy chance that our first visit fell on Nehru's birthday according to the Indian calendar, which is based on the twelve lunar months, so that we were able to share the family's birthday lunch. On that day, symbolically, all the food at their table is Indian.

Going up with Nehru to his den to talk I found its walls completely lined with bookshelves with one or two open parcels of the newest books from England and America on the floor. These included not only some of the most recent books on social and economic problems but a volume of Ernst Toller's plays and the latest novel by Charles Morgan. I opened with the question that had come up in conversation with the doctor met in Calcutta who had been physician to Nehru's father as well as to himself and had also often attended Gandhi. Dr. B. C. Roy in a fascinating conversation, in which he compared the whole philosophy and approach of Gandhi and Nehru, had said, 'the country is anxious now to develop itself in the direction of the constructive and not the destructive revolution'. This point was central with Dr. Roy, who expressed the conviction that a talk which he had for two hours with Gandhi on March 18th, 1934, on the constructive revolution had played a leading part in helping Gandhi to his decision to give up civil disobedience and to issue his programme of village development.

I put to Nehru the question whether in his mind this transition was a real one, that is, to go back to Dr. Roy's own talk, the building up of India's life from below and not simply the destruction of the governmental machine above, the development and organization of the masses of the people. As Dr. Roy said, 'we want to know how to develop ourselves, not to feed upon the iniquities of others but to shed from ourselves the weaknesses and drawbacks that are the cause of our political state'. This, as Dr. Roy explained in response to questioning, does not mean simply the demand of the moderates for alteration within the present scheme but a complete change in the situation initiated by India herself.

Nehru's uncompromising mind came straight out in response to my question. 'That *is* our goal,' he replied, 'but when in your constructive activity you come right up against a blank brick wall you must remove the wall.' 'Britain', he said, 'has, of course, brought many revolutionary things into India including not only ideas of political freedom but railways which are very revolutionary. But having brought in these revolutionary influences the English people always try to stop them from effecting their logical result.'

I asked what would he do, given self-government, in order to create a concrete programme of transformation; and, in addition, was it not possible to get some picture of that constructive change even with the British on the spot? He said that Congress was working at the project of taking a district of India and making a survey of its whole life, discovering its rural, engineering, and educational needs. He criticized the Agricultural Commission survey known as the Linlithgow Report (which I had mentioned as an example of that very thing) with the objection that its terms of reference accepted the existing land tenure system. 'If you accept an evil thing as a permanent part of the landscape, you cannot survey for a constructive revolution', he said. He dismissed the Report of the Commission on Unemployment associated with the name of Sir Tej Bahadur Sapru on the ground that here again all its recommendations were tied up with leaving the existing order unchanged. It was an odd thing, he admitted, in relation to the Sapru report, that only in notes added at the end was there a hint of the big problem; and those notes were by a conservative British commercial man and an English civil servant.

He here made a penetrating distinction between the Indian Liberal mind and the contemporary English Liberal of the type of Ernest Barker or Lord Lothian. 'The Saprus and their like in India do not see,' he said, 'as do the English, the new implications of a transformed economic order.' My own talk with Sir Tej Bahadur Sapru, with whom I raised these very issues, showed his mind to be irrevocably closed against changes that I had regarded as having been accepted, whether reluctantly or gladly, by practically every social and economic thinker in the western world.

I asked Nehru what he felt about the obviously rapidly developing industrialism in India with its capitalistic foundations. He said that India was in the strange position of developing capitalism at the very time when capitalism was in rapid decay in all the lands of its origin. I asked him what parallels he saw in such a situation that faced the peasant population and the smaller but growing industrial proletariat and the position in Russia when the Bolshevik revolution emerged. He said that it had been seen twice in India that when a big revolutionary movement starts it spreads like wildfire. This had happened in 1922 and in 1931. The peasant in India as everywhere else normally thinks in narrow terms of local pressure, but individual peasants in increasing numbers are feeling themselves to be part of some big movement that they connect with socialism. 'In India', he said, and he made another of his penetrating observations in world perspective, 'in India people's minds are changing much more quickly than are the life and external activity of the land. The exact contrary is true of Europe and America, where the whole social and economic life is swiftly changing and people's minds lag behind. The English', he went on, 'everywhere ally themselves with the feudal elements in society. The zemindar system in India is really the creation of the British. The Viceroy is of the landlord class in England and therefore he makes landlords here in India, partly because he knows how to handle them and still more because it is easier to deal with and control a few men than masses. Similarly, the Indian princes and their states are sustained by the British. With the exception of more enlightened states like Mysore,' he continued, 'these despotisms would be knocked down by their subjects if left to themselves; and in North and Central India the native states are pure despotisms. Similarly the landlords would disappear in a peasant proprietorship.'

Coming back to the contrast with Russia he pointed out how much more thickly populated India is, with a very much more complicated land system. Half India has a tenant proprietor of what Russia would call the *tulah* type. He owns his bit of land under the state and his condition is better than that of the tenant under the zemindar. He is now feeling the pinch of a reduced market and cheaper price for his products. He is restless.

From all my talk with Nehru I brought away the clear impression that his essential hatred is of exploitation and imperialism wherever he sees them, that oppression is the vital thing to fight whether the oppressor is a zemindar, an Indian prince or the British Government, a capitalist factory or a millowner, whether he be Parsi, Hindu, or European. He equally sees that the new imperialisms of Japan or Italy and the new repression of liberty in the Nazi or the Fascist state are as hostile to his ideal of life as are the old imperialisms in Asia of Britain or France.

I watched his oval sensitive face as he talked, his dark hair beginning to go grey. While the eyes and the expression as he thought out the answer to some question were meditative, it was the quiet of the smoothly working intellect, not the brooding of the mystic that was in process. An almost passionate determination, a sense of deep wells of emotion, lurked behind the stillness. Here it would seem was a mettlesome thoroughbred war-horse scenting the battle afar off, and only held in check by the disciplined will of the man. While reading the autobiography it had flashed into my mind that here was a personality that combined Prince Rupert with Hamlet. A talk with Nehru intensified this impression. Here was the dashing cavalier eager for the swift charge into the ranks of the enemy, daring, careless of personal peril or discomfort, sometimes indeed likely to charge so far ahead as to lose contact with the ranks he leads. Side by side with him lives the Prince of Denmark, the man who in a deep brooding melancholy can cry, 'The time is out of joint:—O cursèd spite, that ever I was born to set it right'; the man who feels within himself the tug of the West, the leaven of Harrow and Cambridge which, as he himself has said, makes him feel always an exile in India, and yet with something unconquerably Indian within him which will never let him be an essential part of the West. Nehru has the statesman's gift for long perspectives, but he has not Gandhi's intuition for dramatizing his actions or feeling the pulse of the vast illiterate masses. Temperamentally an aristocrat he is, with all his passionate socialism, incapable of either looking or even, it would seem, feeling himself one of the people. Saturated in the culture of the West, he never gives the impression that Gandhi always conveys of being of the very soil of India. That touch of brooding aloofness, even when he is thronged by thousands of students or some vast city crowd, ever refuses to let him become, in the curious sense that is so true of Gandhi, a part of that Indian crowd. Perhaps this is intensified by his Indian robe which, as he wears it, inevitably recalls a young Roman senator in his toga. He is the only man I have seen on whom the *khaddar* cap, worn by all the devotees of Congress, becomes something princely.

Talking with Mr. P. Mahadevan, the Hindu Principal of Madura College, about Nehru, who was speaking in Madura at that very time, he said: 'He feels with the skin of an Englishman. He has a terrible task. The great gift of Nehru to India at this time is to give us an intellectual justification of the movement for independence. Just as Stalin and Lenin, the men of blood and iron, were the products of the thinker, Karl Marx, so it may possibly come to be with us in India. Nehru is there to clarify and to make an intellectual study of the next step. He seeks to give a basis for the movement as a coherent fight against exploitation. In doing this he lifts the conflict above the question of race, because he is as much an enemy of the Indian capitalist who exploits the poor as he is of the British government. Indeed, you may have noticed that a number of Indian newspapers are more vehement in their attacks upon Nehru than are the English newspapers.'

One element in what one can almost call the tragedy of Jawaharlal Nehru is that an unswerving idealist wedded to an uncompromising doctrine of revolution is supreme younger leader of a Congress that is bourgeois and has been financed by Indian industrialists and zemindars, the very people whom the logical expression of his doctrine would eliminate. He has, it is certain, given such offence to numbers of these as to lessen the party funds. His answer to this is to widen the range of appeal. To an outsider it would seem as though both sides were playing for time. The Congress Socialist party has grown rapidly, and an increasing number, especially of the younger delegates, stand solidly behind him. Will the time come when that party will be so dominant that Nehru can force the issue? Then a split must follow; and the landlords and millowners will swerve toward the British government, while the intellectuals, the peasants, and the workers will hear a surer and more resonant note of social revolution. On the other side, the bourgeois capitalist elements in Congress may hope that time will wear down the uncompromising socialism of Nehru.

As I talked with Nehru the feeling grew that his real burning fury, so far as persons are concerned, is not against the British but against what he calls 'the lapdog type of Indian', who, as a time-serving sneak, or purely as an ambitious opportunist, fawns on the British rule which in his heart he hates. Insincerity is to him the ultimate enemy.

The impression made by Jawaharlal Nehru on an Indian seer of the experience and penetration of Tagore deeply interested me. Rabindranath Tagore had been talking to me about the entirely disheartening effect on himself of the intensification of Hindu-Muslim communal antagonisms, due in his view to the communal award of the British government integrated into the new constitution. 'Nehru', he said, 'is not so pessimistic as I am. To him the younger generation turns. He has the spirit of truth; he is absolutely honest. He has captured the heart of India. He is so outspoken. The smaller breed of politicians think that lies are needed, but we have found in him the true leader, ready to fight against odds with resources however small.'

It is here that we come on that strange blend of emotions that burns in Nehru as he stands face to face with Gandhi. They differ as the poles asunder on religion, on economics, and on social theory. Gandhi becomes quite clearly more profoundly Hindu every year and his mystical confidence in spiritual forces deepens; while Nehru has the western scientific mind and sees forces working in the cold light of reason. He frankly has no use for institutional religion, and shares with millions of Indians the loathing of those loyalties that lead to communal conflict. But he goes further and is unable to assent to any spiritual explanation of the universe. Yet I have never met a man over whom moral ideas appear to have more absolute authority. Christians who would condemn a man on the ground of his lack of religious faith have cause to hesitate long enough to ask what bearing Jesus' parable of the Judgement has as we confront a man who has suffered prison repeatedly and for years for his ideal of freeing and raising his people. I suppose few of us would be certain that we could stand so searching a test.

When Nehru broke with his careless life of hunting and social enjoyment years ago his conversion—for no other word is adequate—came through devotion to Gandhi. To-day he is far from being a disciple of Gandhi in the sense of accepting his teaching, but he gives to him a free affectionate devotion, and often carries out his wishes even when they do not accord with his own judgement. He perpetually acclaims him as the leader under whom the inert masses of India have developed habits of co-operative action, of self-respect, and the straight back in place of the cringing stoop. The free colleagueship of women in public life, the growth of a wider outlook, the unique spread of political and economic discussion, and the remarkable transformation in the masses, which Nehru regards as the only foundation on which a stable structure can be built, he credits to the vision and courage and intuitive genius of Gandhi's leadership. So we face this strange alliance of two men who would appear to differ in almost every essential except in the common goal of freeing India from British rule.

As I stood on the balcony outside Nehru's den looking across the India where Britain has ruled now for so long there surged across me the maddening dilemma in which we all stand who love India. I could build up such a catalogue of Britain's blunders and crimes, collective and individual, as might rival even those of a Congress Nationalist, yet at the end of the day I would have to ask myself two things. First, does a Nehru or a Gandhi ever realistically envisage the Himalayan immensity and complexity of the task that awaits any new government? There has never been in all history nor is there to-day anywhere on this planet a problem comparable to the rule of a sixth of the human family, hag-ridden by stupendous inertia, weighed down both by the spiritual sanctions of *karma* and the physical sapping lethargies of malaria, hookworm, under-feeding and evil feeding, child marriage and other pestilencies. In this India to-day inter-provincial animosities affect economic, political, and every other activity of life, and her whole life is confessed by every honest observer to be dragged down by the immemorial traditions of using power for family advancement and the making of money out of the holding of office. It is because I passionately sympathize with the desire of India for self-rule that I feel almost a personal sense of agony at the angry refusal of the vast majority of Indian Nationalists to look straight into the face of this colossal issue and frame some policy to grapple with it. The answer given every time is that nothing can be done while the British are there. Then I contemplate such a fact as that Britain has made over seventy-five thousand miles of canals in India—somewhat more than twice the amount of irrigation in the United States of America, so that fifty million people are employed on land that was formerly desert or uncultivable—and that this irrigation with the creation of transport by rail and road has made famine for ever impossible for the first time in India's history. Then, on the other side, Indians confess to me that the peasant farmer cannot get his quota of water from those canals without oiling the hands of the Indian petty official in charge—and I cannot but believe that the recognition of such facts frankly and fully would in the long run strengthen the Nationalist hand.

Repeated talks and discussions running through whole days with man after man, often of first-class legal training and graduation with the highest honours in western universities, who are worked up to such intense fury by British rule that they cannot think of anything but how to get rid of it, have driven me to the conviction that there is no solution to this problem in the light of reason. As one of the greatest of them said, 'It is this atmosphere that has strangled and suffocated us and made it almost impossible for us to consider anything but the hands at our throats and the foul air we have to breathe. Insult and injury have been heaped on those we cherish, while everything that is evil and bad in India has been encouraged and fostered.' These words from the lips of a man of towering ability and scholarship, words that, while they accurately describe his emotions, seem fantastic in their exaggeration and lop-sidedness as a description of British rule, convince me that it is only by Britain taking on her shoulders the responsibility of a great gesture of renunciation that this furious emotional complex can be eliminated and co-operation reached.

This brings me to the second conundrum of which I have never yet reached a convincing solution. Perhaps there is none. If the smoke from the smouldering emotional fury disappeared, would a Nehru in the clear cold light of realism and logic believe in or even see as desirable the absolute break with Britain that his passion now demands?

Numerous voices, some Indian as well as more British, have expressed the conviction that for Congress to achieve its goal and be saddled with the rule of India would be 'to be found out'. In other words, that it is really bankrupt of power to implement its own goal if achieved, and, deeper and more searching still, that the leaders of Congress know this to be so. If this were true, then psychologically it might go far to explain the fury, for calm assurance of capacity is not prone to 'see red'. On the other side that fury could, in part at any rate, be the result not only of that lack of trust that the safeguards in the new constitution suggest, but much more the knowledge that in any considerable group of students some government spy is among them, that others are eavesdropping in factories, creeping through caravanserais and bazaars and all too often evincing that strange loathsome blend of cunning, crass stupidity and maddening arrogance which is the unique achievement of the mind of the underworld of the governmental spy system.

As I rose to take leave of Nehru after our third talk he took up the slim volume of his earliest letters to his daughter, Indira, and then the two plump volumes of letters to her that filled the fifteen hundred pages of his *Glimpses of World History* and inscribed them to me as from one writer to another. He did it all with that simplicity and charm which makes him one of the half-dozen most attractive personalities I have ever met. The translucent unforced sincerity that does not know how to do anything else than express lucidly the thought that is in him had captured me. And as I read his limpid prose, rising again and again with complete naturalness to heights that make it pure literature, I am driven to wonder whether some day his immortal niche in the world's temple will be carved more by his pen than by his statecraft. His letters from prison and his books were written with *swadeshi* ink on *swadeshi* paper, but the brain that moved his pen is that of a world citizen, who, as we talked, lifted each subject into a world perspective. Destiny has surely worked more unlikely paradoxes than that some fine day this man should, in a world where the frenzy of nationalist and imperialist dictatorships shall have passed away, sit in Westminster or Geneva, helping to weave the fabric of a new world comity of peoples.

CHAPTER V

Renaissance under Alien Rule

ANY searcher for trends toward a new India is bound to have his eye on signs of cultural renaissance. The problem as to how far a Robert Burns was the cause and how far the effect of a new Scottish consciousness, or how far the new national poetry was a creative flame in the nineteenth-century fire of Finnish nationalism can, I suppose, never be determined. How far, again, did the Renaissance in Florence or Venice depend on the accident of brilliant genius coinciding with the patronage of princes avid of glory, and how far was it due to the release into the European world of classical Greek literature exiled from Constantinople by the invading Turk? To sit in an Indian city like Madura or Mysore, Calcutta or Lahore, is to realize suddenly that these questions I have just put are not academic but very actual. English literature injected into India has had effects oddly parallel to, on the one hand, the Latin that was the lingua franca of medieval Europe, and on the other hand, the Greek which was the Renaissance medium of new ideas. Similarly, again, the poetry of a Sir Mohammed Iqbal in the Islamic North, or of a Rabindranath Tagore in Bengal, great as it is as a literary event, is still more potent as sounding a réveillé.

When, therefore, I asked an eminent and cultured Indian judge in Madura the question as to what signs there are of a cultural renaissance in the Tamil world of South India, the interest was deeper than that of literature. In an incautious moment I put the question in the challenging form that I had heard much of the cultural renaissance of Bengal but nothing of that in the Tamil-speaking world. He answered, 'Yes, the Bengali is good at self-advertisement. He has learned it from the West.' This humorous shaft having duly gone home, I waited for more constructive knowledge. But there was little that was concrete or coherent. A fervid poet, Bahrita, whose books were earlier on suppressed by the provincial government, quickened the nationalist pulses of the people who sang his lyrics—but he is dead. The judge, who is a Hindu, and a learned theosophist who was staying with him told me of many poems and essays appearing in many Tamil periodicals, all of them symptoms of something about to be given to the world, but neither coherent enough to be a movement nor vigorous enough to make a stir. The judge then asked, how can a strong cultural renaissance grow up under a cold-blooded, soulless bureaucracy directed by an alien government having no root in the soil of India? Renaissance, as he pointed out, has depended so often on the patronage of rulers who, desiring beautiful buildings, needed architects, and in furnishing them needed sculptors and painters, and whose personal renown was spread by court poets and historians.

'Music', he said, 'is the one Indian art that has never gone into ruin and has kept alive the old traditions. The decorative arts and crafts are being ruined by industrialism, and the finer minds are being drawn into active politics. The one beautiful building in Madura was built when there was a king in Madras, a patron of the arts and crafts.'

Another vivid point of view was expressed from a

totally different angle by a retired civil servant of Tamil birth, who confessed that he now reads practically nothing but English; for, so he said, what is called Tamil literature is only the clumsy expression of western ideas in unintelligible Tamil.

So I turned my face toward the Bengali renaissance. Mr. A. C. Chakravarty, at Oxford and in London, had given me some picture of what is going on in Bengal. He himself, a brilliant littérateur, combines his discipleship of Rabindranath Tagore with genuine critical independence of outlook. He spoke to me of the hunger of young men in Bengal for a breath of the cultural life of the greater world. He himself was, interestingly enough, engaged at Balliol in completing a thesis for a doctorate of literature on English mentality as revealed in its post-war poetry, impervious to the gibes of some of the older dwellers on Olympus who insist that there *is* no mentality in post-war poetry.

I set out on a pilgrimage to the venerable seer who is always referred to quite simply throughout Bengal as 'the Poet'. I went in a sufficiently humble frame of mind, remembering that years ago, when I called on Rabindranath Tagore in Kensington to ask him for unpublished poems to produce in a magazine, the window from which he looked out gave directly upon that apotheosis of Victorian ugliness born of sentimentality and a false conception of art, the Albert Memorial. I found that across the years he recalled the view of that atrocity. The poet, whose shoulders have begun to stoop a little, but whose eye still quickens with its ancient fire, made eager and affectionate inquiries for his disciple and secretary, Chakravarty. There was something at once beautiful and pathetic in the intensity of his regard for the younger generation through whom his creative impulses can continue to find expression.

Tagore was in his little simple country house to which he retires in vacation time, living in just a single room with a large balcony reached by a narrow spiral stair. On his table on the balcony was the new collected edition of his poems that had just reached him from Macmillan. When I asked him if he were continuing to write he replied that writing was a gift he was sent to employ. Critical voices had told me in advance in India that he was tending more and more to desire adulation. Our talk gave the eloquent lie to that, for he turned aside from talk of himself to sing the praises of Gandhi and Nehru, to plead the cause of the détenus, and to sound the trumpet of rural reconstruction. Of this aspect of my talk with him we shall speak later. He was emphatic, however, that no development of rural reconstruction is possible without a cultural background. 'Village life', he said, 'is a whole life. The development of scientific technique by itself will not build a new village India. The spirit must be lifted and formed.'

As I left him and went round the wide acreage of Santiniketan, the school of the arts and cultures that his enthusiasm and genius have created, with persons not buildings as the centre of interest, the knowledge that something real was being achieved there came, for example, most of all through instances like the following. I strolled round the corner of a simple students' hostel and looked into one of the cells that is the living-room and bedroom of each student. On a mat under the light of the single window a student sat with a board on his knees, stooping over it completely absorbed in what I could see at a glance was a piece of pure creative art.

I stood watching him for several minutes, but he was completely unconscious of anything in the world save the beauty that he was striving to release. Just outside the hostel was a work of art whose grip I still cannot explain. It is called 'The milkmaid', and is roughly moulded by hand from rough-cast cement. My intellect tells me that a figure twice the height of a girl yet thinner than any maid could be cannot be a true presentation of personality; but my eye tells me that my reasoning is wrong. She stands there, erect, with a jar upon her head, poised in arrested motion. It is the creation, not of any outstanding genius, but the free expression of a student. On the outer walls of half the buildings of Santiniketan are mural paintings done by students, revealing the curiously potent unsuspected creative talent that lies in so many of us waiting to be released. As I watched this joy of youth in self-expression and contrasted it with the forces that had driven precisely similar young men to terrorism with bomb and pistol, my mind went back to words that Rabindranath Tagore had spoken an hour earlier: 'I employed some young men to help the villages in rural reconstruction. Before I left I saw the government people and said that the boys were there to build up a new atmosphere for villages. When I came back I found every one of them in jail. Maybe before they joined me they had revolutionary aims, but they all promised me to do nothing revolutionary. Once, however, a man is suspected by the police he is doomed for ever. When those boys came back from prison they were crushed in spirit and in health. When people ask what has happened to Bengal I say, "The real Bengal is in jail".' Whether or not Tagore had been mistaken in his confidence in those young men, the principle on which he acted—the education of the emotions and the harnessing them along with the mind to creative work—is valid. That is the principle on which the whole of his educational work at Santiniketan is based. It will be a calamity if, when Tagore, as must be the case, passes out of control, the direction of Santiniketan should come into hands less strong in their grasp of this great truth to which, in the West, adventurous thinkers in philosophy and religion like John Macmurray, and experimental psychologists like Dr. Madge Lowenfeld, are just leading us. It seemed to me that where weakness reveals itself in Santiniketan it is at the points where the examination demands for degrees in the great universities have forced Tagore's school to deflect its programme to that end.

So far the pernicious influence of a degree of a certain type being necessary if a man is to get employment, and that degree being dependent on cramming from text-books, has been too powerful for Santiniketan altogether to resist. There are few students who can afford to ignore the necessity of earning their living when their course is over. A minority only see the possibility of launching out into separate creative writing, painting, sculpture, weaving, farming, or wood-handicraft on a scale adequate for livelihood. In one sense we see here an example supporting the thesis that my Madura friend put forward, of the cramping effect of an alien rule, particularly through its educational system, on indigenous culture. It is an odd paradox that the western educational development that has flowered from Macaulay's Minute simultaneously made a Tagore possible and set obstacles in the way of the creative cultural synthesis that is his goal.

Leaving Santiniketan to go back to share the fellowship of the young cultural group that is working toward a new literature in Bengali, I found that I was not turning my back on Rabindranath Tagore, for I met a group of eager adventurous young intellectuals who, the more enthusiastically they explore the new creations of western poetry, become more profoundly filled with wondering reverence for their great Bengali seer-poet. They declared that Tagore is in some ways more modern than many younger men. He succeeds in being modern, they said, because for one thing he is better equipped than most people, and secondly, he knows what you can be modern about. They mentioned a recent book of his in fictional form in Bengali dealing with terrorism. It is full, also, of love interest. Tagore's own Bengali technique, they declared, is quite perfect, marvellous in its rhythmic beauty.

His English poetry, they said, is not really to be compared with that in Bengali. This raised in my mind the question that was to be sharply thrown into relief later in Mysore by Professor Wadia. It arises out of the paradox that when patriotism in India leads a man to produce literature in his native tongue, what he really strengthens is provincialism. Sir Mohammed Iqbal, the Muslim poet in Lahore, learned in Urdu and Persian, or a Tamil poet in Madras or Madura, is as sharply cut off from the stimulus of Tagore's Bengali poetry as I am myself. If these local cultural developments intensify, shall we possibly have a situation paralleling that of the transition from medieval to modern Europe, when they lost the lingua franca of Latin and developed out of what were dialects a German, a French, an Italian, and an English literary medium? Shall we in the India of to-morrow, as in the Europe of the Renaissance, experience simultaneously a gain in literature but a loss in catholicity of spirit? I was astonished to realize from a talk with the Parachiya group that Bengali written prose is now barely a hundred years old.

I talked with one after another of the group as they wandered into the book-lined salon-study where their leader, Dr. Dutt, works. Most of them wore the crisp white dhoti, with its flowing lines, and a plain white tunic reaching almost to the knees. Here was a young professor, there a young official writing poetry in his leisure time, another turned out to be a novelist, one even was introduced as a champion wrestler.

I asked whether there is any new poetry in Bengali parallel to Carl Sandberg's praises of iron and steel and mechanism; or, alternatively, to that of the new western communist poets. Much experiment is being made, I was told, but nothing of much importance has yet been written. In prose these things can be handled, they said, because the use of practically English words, especially in talk of machines or of new social theories, does not create a difficulty; but the close-knit texture of Bengali verse and its dependence upon the aura around words makes lyrics about machinery practically impossible at present. With regard to the poetry of communism, they declared that the pressure of censorship in Bengal made rebel poetry taboo. The tendency is growing up to write a cadenced prose that is not quite *vers libre.*

I put a further question as to whether modern drama was being produced in Bengali. The reply again from one man was that this is immensely difficult because there is little social intercourse, relatively speaking, between the sexes. The generalization was challenged, as it well might be, on at least two grounds. There is a continuous movement toward fuller relationship in social life between men and women in India. Not only can those relationships be subject to drama, but actually the tension involved in moving from the old separated life to that of social relationships in itself creates drama. Secondly, the western stage is continuously witnessing plays that place no reliance on the drama of relations between men and women, as shown, e.g. from Bernard Shaw's *St. Joan* to Hugh Walpole's *The Old Ladies* and Obey's *Noah*.

The development of social life between men and women is having a curious influence on fictional literature in Bengal. When fiction began to be written in Bengali in the middle of the nineteenth century, it modelled itself on the contemporary European novel. The Bengali novel was thus romantic and utterly unrelated to Indian life. To-day the difference between the actual social situation and that portrayed in novels is far less, because of the freer human relationships. One of the difficulties, they told me, of writing Bengali novels is that in real life the conversation of cultivated people, men and women alike, drops unconsciously into English to express modern ideas. As a result, conversation in a Bengali novel tends to become stilted. I gathered that one of the great contributions of the leader of the Parachiya group, Dr. Dutt, lies in the actual creative introduction of fresh words in Bengali, which this young group is convinced is an essential process if the language is to hold its own in expressing the ideas and the ideals of young modern Indian life. The writing of fiction is not a career for a person in search of a livelihood in Bengal. A 'best-seller' may dispose of an edition of 500 copies in the first year or of 1,000 in ten years.

The group condemned the Indian cinema as utterly futile. My own subsequent experience makes me wish to go back to them and challenge them to further discussion on that issue, which is momentous for the future. I saw three Indian films in India under expert guidance. The first two completely merited the group's description of futile. Photographically feeble and scenically second-rate, their structure was fatuous beyond the dreams even of Hollywood. Each of them seemed to be made on a brainless mechanical formula, derivative from the western film at its worst. In this type of film you must have chase over hill and dale and cross-roads, first on horseback and then in cars; there must be knockabout farce of the crudest type; equally crude writhing dances of the type associated with New York burlesque; romantic sword-and-cloak fighting in dungeons or over castle walls, and long-drawn kisses; punctuated throughout with singing to pseudo-Indian music at astoundingly inappropriate moments. One of these films, with Indian actors and actresses in a scene laid at the court of an Indian state but with alarms and excursions in all directions, was drawn out from ten p.m. to one o'clock in the morning.

The third film, however, seen at Bombay, was beautifully photographed, scenically appropriate and interesting, and possessed a coherent plot with sustained interest cumulatively to the climax. Oddly enough, it might in one sense be called a propaganda film, for it was centred from first to last on a passionate advocacy of rural reconstruction. But this very intensity of purpose served it artistically, just as it does, for example, in

Galsworthy's *Justice* or *The Silver Box*. The outline of its plot illustrates so appropriately the theme of rural reconstruction that I shall detail it in Chapter X. The urgent question that it raises in my mind for the cultural future of India is whether young Indian writers and artists, even though inhibited from the extremer social and political fields, cannot discover in these conflicts between the old and new ways and in the tensions between cynicism and idealism the very stuff of drama. It is significant that in Bombay alone, while this film was being shown to crowded houses week after week, three other films, all handling dramatically parallel themes, were being simultaneously and successfully produced in the city. Is it not possible that these experiments in the newer medium of the film may have a lesson for adventurous cultural groups in India toward a literature that flowers out of life and in doing so yields the fruit of a new society?

In India the P.E.N. Club has two centres, one led by Dr. Kalidas Nag at Calcutta, the other in Bombay—the parent Indian group—with Madam Sophia Wadia as its secretary. In both places the club was called together so that I might meet its members. In each case I felt that their present contribution to India lies in keeping open to the cultural breezes of the world the windows of a land whose vehement nationalism at times tends to close the shutters. This was illustrated by the fact that Madam Wadia and Dr. Nag had just returned from the International Congress of the P.E.N. Club in Latin America; and is true also to the genius of this organization, whose centres in most of the countries of the world exist mainly to bring writers from other lands into fellowship with their fellow craftsmen.

To me, two exciting enigmas raise their heads here for an answer that only the future can give. May it be that when the association of English with an alien government is a thing of the past, that language may really become a main medium of Indian thought? As I read, for instance, Nehru's *Autobiography* and Sarojini Naidu's lyrics, I feel that here their minds and spirits work to use English not because it is a convenient medium of expression that will reach a wider world, but because it is spiritually and emotionally wedded most intimately to the feelings and ideas within them. Both of these writers, be it noted, are passionately national. If we think of Ireland as a parallel, one asks whether it is possible that in Erse there can be any literature burning with a purer, whiter flame of the Irish spirit than the poems of Yeats and Padraic Colum, the prose of A. E., and the drama of Synge.

The second enigma asked whether, as English becomes more and more essentially indigenous in India, India herself may not enrich it immeasurably for the rest of the English-speaking world, not simply of the Empire but of America, by the continuous introduction of fresh ways of expression, infiltrated from the eastern mind as well as from the languages themselves. When the boy Kim, having played truant, asks that 'the hand of friendship may put aside the whip of calamity', Kipling's phrase is such as could never have come save through the medium of the East.

CHAPTER VI

City of Pilgrims

As we climbed from the river boat up the steps of one of the many bathing ghats of Benares, a shrill harsh medley of sounds cascaded towards us. A troop of half-starved monkeys fighting for a scrap of food would have made just such an ungodly clamour. Looking up I saw a shrinking pilgrim trying to make his way down the narrow alley to reach the waters of the sacred river. Like sharks the waiting hordes precipitated themselves on him, shouting 'backsheesh' with extended hand and grasping claw. This was the greeting of Benares to one of the million pilgrims who every year seek enlightenment or healing, or come to lay their bones in the sacred city, for to die within its walls means immediate transport to paradise.

It came on me with a shock to recall that for over a quarter of a century Benares was the first and Florence the second of the two cities I had most of all wanted to see in the whole world. Thinking of Benares my mind had always been filled with a vision of pilgrims trailing along the highways of India, the glow of a quest in their eyes and a spiritual hunger in their hearts; with the feeling of the slow eternal lapse of the mighty river; with the knowledge that probably for some three thousand years men had come to its banks for a vision of the Eternal, as Sakyamuni the Buddha came five centuries before the birth of Christ. This had been the Benares of my dreams, and here I seemed to be walking in a den of thieves and robbers.

As we walked along the narrow stench-ridden alleyways from the ghats to the city, the path was one unbroken string of begging bowls held aloft with beseeching hands by women, most of them dressed in the coarse white garment of the widow. And as I looked into temple after temple, the pilgrim was paying the sleek priests. The words of the Jat farmer with his sick child when he met Kim came back to me:

> 'The priests tell us that Benares is holy—which none doubt—and desirable to die in. But I do not know their Gods, and they ask for money; and when one has done one worship the shaved-head vows it is of none effect except one do another. Wash here! Wash there! Pour, drink, lave, and scatter flowers—but always pay the priests.'

In almost violent contrast with the timorous pilgrim trying to elude the human sharks and dip his hands in the holy waters was the arrogant fakir. Thrusting aside the clutching hands of the beggars and shouldering by the ordinary pilgrim, he swaggered to his prominent place of meditation.

Pushing past the almost intimidating begging-bowls thrust menacingly in our faces, we climbed the stone steps of a house, guided by the sound of women's voices singing Indian lyrics. Holding the nose, we slipped by evil-smelling latrines, and at a doorway our eyes rested on a strange sight. A hall, rather dimly lighted by stained-glass windows, was completely filled with women seated on the floor, all singing continuously, led by one who stood in front of them. They were chanting the graces of the gods. The songs go on day and night incessantly by relays of Hindu widows, who are rewarded for their service out of a legacy left by a rich devotee. As we looked across the shaven heads of these women, dressed in the one coarse white garment prescribed by custom and bereft of all the jewellery so dear to the Indian woman's heart, we saw the rapt devotion on the faces of many. The wonderful place music has in the soul-life of India made another of its multitudinous impressions upon me. I took a time-exposure photograph of the interior. Not one woman noticed our presence, and all the outlines are quite clear, so still and absorbed were they.

The tall pencils of two solitary minarets, rising as it seemed above the very walls of Hindu temples, were a lively reminder of two startling facts about Benares. The first is that with the coming of a lieutenant of Gazni the Idol Smasher who conquered Benares, and later in the twelfth century of the Emperor Allah-ud-Din, a thousand Hindu temples were utterly destroyed and mosques built in their place. Even in the central citadel of Hinduism the ferocious idol-loathing puritanism of Islam was not quelled; but to-day—and this is the greater lesson still—only one mosque survives on the water-front. The slow irresistible absorptive power of Hinduism has once more asserted itself. There is no more vital and disputed question for the future of India than the enigma, can Hinduism survive the corrosions of the most potent enemy that it has yet faced—the acids of the scientific mind and the remorseless drive of the machines of the twentieth century?

Going quietly along the water-front, watching the devout gestures of the bathing pilgrims in what is, I suppose, one of the most exquisite symbolic rites that the world knows, as sun and water are hailed as divine sources of energy and cleansing, I caught glimpses of some of the deep sources of the strength of Hinduism. Watching those ash-smeared fakirs, the immense appeal of the spiritual quest became apparent. Some of them I knew to be men of wonderful attainments in learning —I heard of one, for instance, who was master of eight languages—some of them had been trained in western universities and now all were Seekers of the Way. Behind the thrusting and truculent impostors and the vampire horde of clamorous beggars the music of the universal chant of unsatisfied longing for God began to be heard. I could almost see Kim's lama striding toward the Tirthanker temple of the Jains to tell his beads in Benares in the intervals of his unceasing quest for the River of the Arrow.

Our companion on this pilgrimage had himself been a Hindu seeker, a man who had graduated with honours in philosophy. His enlightenment had come many years before in the face of Jesus Christ. As we strolled among the pilgrims he held in his hand a bunch of leaflets. One and another would stop him in the Indian manner and ask what he held there. His answer would sometimes lead to friendly discussion, sometimes to scornful heckling, and again, at times, to the purchase of one of the little books, most of them translations of the Gospels into the main Indian languages, which he carried in a bag. It was one of the fascinating elements in this process that Mr. Das needed to size up the place of origin of his questioner and to have acquaintance with numerous languages to deal with these pilgrims from all parts of the sub-continent of India. He told us, too, that year by year the attitude of the Hindu pilgrims to himself and his Christian good news is more open, and often he is listened to in the friendly spirit proper to the true seeker.

Any one familiar with the cheerful jostling crowds of the Indian streets, with their delightful readiness to ask and answer questions of all and sundry, will realize that this method, which would mean thrusting unwilling attention on absorbed hurrying business people in a London street, is natural and normal in an Indian city, especially one where pilgrims gather. These conversations again and again led to an invitation by Mr. Das to a pilgrim to come round later in the day and hear a lecture and join in discussion in his little depot near the top of the ghat steps.

As we went back through the streets of Benares into the business quarter, on a raised veranda by the thronged street sat an Englishman with a dense thatch of silvery hair and irresistible laughing eyes set in a rosy face. As business men, shopkeepers, and pilgrims see J. C. Jackson sitting there, they come to him as to a *guru*. A shrewd, humorous Christian saint, with some forty years' experience, side by side with his Indian wife whose character might have come straight out of the Acts of the Apostles, he is uniquely equipped for entering into the heart of the intimate problems of an Indian and seeing the answer that is true at once to reality and to the man's need.

On the roadside, remote from the houses of caste Hindus, yet within Benares municipality, lay an open dusty space over which sprawled crazy huts. Children looked out under a tangle of matted hair at the strangers. We were walking among the hovels of an outcaste group, the Doms. Thrust down into the mud, under the feet of Hinduism, denied legitimate access even to the sheer necessities of life, they are by profession thieves. The first reaction of the western mind to the thought of theft is of individuals with a sense of guilt plotting robbery. But the social structure in India has through the ages created these groups among whom successful theft and other crimes are matters for pride. The mass education within the group is directed to that end. The civic rule of Benares ignores them when it comes to providing sanitation, lighting, or roads. The interest of governmental authority in them is at some point in the night to make a roll-call of the group. Each individual, at whatever hour the call is made, must come out of his slumbers and answer to his name. A failure to respond means a month in prison; a second failure a longer term, and a third a period up to a year. The aim, of course, is to protect the citizens of Benares and indeed of a far wider neighbourhood from their raids and maraudings.

Language breaks down and indeed imagination boggles at the effort to grasp and express the sub-human, even, in some ways, sub-animal life of the Doms. For twenty years at least I had heard of them and thought that my mind was prepared to grasp their state, but here were people in a condition far below surly grievance or even the will to be helped. Scarcely a flicker of response can be seen in the great majority of them, even by those who have given years to their service. As I tried to look into their eyes, it seemed as though the age-long denial of any elementary recognition of their humanity had at last drawn a thick veil between them and their fellow men. Only a few years ago they would hide their babies from the white woman who came to minister to them lest she should cut off their ears. Animistic superstition and rites secretly practised, the haunting terror of ghoulish demons, sustained semi-starvation, the cankerous eating of disease into mind as well as body, awed and horrified me into a feeling that here was a hell that not even the imagination of a Dante had envisaged. Spurned so long, their back is turned to life. All over the world the demon-worshipping animist has turned with alacrity to the strange liberation effected by the Christian belief in a Father-God before whose face 'demons fear and fly'. But in the Dom, for the most part, comprehension and response come slowly, as we were told by one who has heroically given the healing and helping hand of the good samaritan to these folks for years. In the little primitive school with its Christian catechist-teacher and the children seated on the ground, dullness and lethargy marked the majority of faces; while on many of them the loathsome marks of venereal disease already showed. I do not expect ever to cease to be haunted by the face of one mother, her face half-eaten away as the result of syphilis, and expecting within a few days to bring into the world a child doomed to life-long misery even before its birth. Behind her in the same settlement was another syphilitic girl of about fourteen, the unmarried mother of two children, she herself not knowing who was the father of either of them. The season when I was walking through these Dom settlements, of which there are nearly a score in Benares, was the best in the year. It was still more appalling to try to conceive what could be the condition of all this filth and disease either in the flaming heat of summer, when the sun's rays beat down like swords, or in the monsoons, when the earth and excreta are churned into a loathsome welter of stinking mud.

As I watched Miss Spencer, who was our guide, open up her dispensing case and give quinine here, apply ointment there, give an injection to kill pain yonder, and arrange to send one terror-stricken woman to hospital; and when I remembered that day in and day out, year after year, she and her colleague, Miss Armstrong, confront the stench and the loathsome sores of these largely unresponsive creatures and love and play with the children, finding them lovable, I felt that I had never seen anything so near to heaven come so close to hell. And not one of the thirty thousand Brahmins in Benares would come within reach of the pollution of even the shadow of these miserable creatures, nor did one of the multitudinous temples open a door for their approach to God. Thousands of priests and Levites of their own countrymen pass by on the other side, while the alien 'heretic' is their good samaritan. Nor does it seem that it can be an accident that those who carry on this work are dedicated to the service of Christ. The lifting of the wounded from the ditch is clearly central to this service; but I have been haunted ever since by the conviction that far more vehement and skilled enterprise must be spent on transforming the system which thus beats and robs them and leaves them for dead.

In a compound I saw a group of Dom boys and girls being led by a Dom Christian teacher in an exquisitely natural rehearsal of a very simple Nativity play. The heart-breaking thing is that they are often taken away after two or three years at school (unhappily a very common practice in India), and one wonders how much permanent impression has been made. In an industrial school I saw adolescent boys being trained to skilled carpenter-craftsmanship, a few Doms among them. I have carried about with me ever since a beautifully turned piece of wood which one of them put on the lathe in its crude form and carved and polished in my presence—a symbol of the transformation that can and does take place. But the redemptive successes cannot blind us to the victims of the stranglehold of evil custom. Behind it all looms the monster problem to which no man has yet suggested a solution for India—what we have already called her 'age-less fecundity'. It seemed impossible to look at those children rotten with disease and not feel convinced that it would have been better for them had they never been born, although we were assured that in many cases they bring great joy to their parents. The skills of the scientist, the psychologist, the sociologist, the economist, must be harnessed to the solution of this apparently insoluble problem, for any project toward its solution, such as sterilization, artificial birth-control, the development of a plan towards a co-operative social order at once raises emotional reactions in many different quarters that paralyse action.

Within a few hours I found myself looking into the eager faces of at least twelve hundred Hindu students gathered in the great hall of their wonderful university. I had tea on the lawn previously with the professors and had enjoyed comparing notes with a man who, as a student at Oxford, had been under the same tutor in the same school of modern history as myself. It was intensely interesting to discuss what use he was making here in the heart of Hinduism of Ernest Barker's political philosophy of the group mind.

I have never spoken to any audience with a livelier zest or a keener eagerness to look through a window opened on world affairs than this rapt assembly of Hindu youth, to whom I talked on 'Youth, the Dictators, and the World Crisis'. Intensely absorbed as they are in their own nationalism, you could see the shock that came to them as they watched youth under the imperialism of Japan and under the dynamic regimentation of Hitler, Mussolini, and Kemal Ataturk. This Hindu University at Benares, with a campus covering an area of two square miles, with two thousand students in its five hostels, opened another window for me on the effort of the progressive wing of Hinduism to justify its all-embracing claims.

A sensational adventure by Hinduism in this direction has crystallized in the new temple to Mother India just outside Benares, which I had visited the same afternoon. On entering the temple, which is surrounded by a continuous cloister, one looks down on surely the strangest object of worship that the world can afford. An enormous relief-map of India, carved in pure carrara marble, lies there surrounded by the Indian Ocean and the Bay of Bengal, with the Himalayas rising majestically to the north. The science and craftsmanship are so perfect that water poured on the Himalayas where the snows melt will run down the river valleys into the seas. The whole map is a perfectly scaled model.

At the opening of the temple, which took place a few months before I reached Benares, the immemorial ceremony of Hinduism was performed by which the spirit is invoked whose presence henceforward makes the hitherto spiritually insignificant marble or stone a god. Into this temple may come the outcastes, to whom most of the other Hindu temples are closed. Thus Hinduism strives to call back into its own fold the youth to whom nationalism has become another religion. Multitudes of politically minded Hindus who are disgusted with the crudities of the pot-bellied elephant-headed Ganesh, the monkey-headed Hanuman, or the ogress Kali, may thus find a spiritual home in one of Hinduism's many mansions.

The temple was built by a wealthy Hindu, Shiva Prasad Gupta, a devotee of Gandhi and an enthusiastic nationalist, who is the proprietor of a vehemently patriotic daily paper called *The Day*. In his home, not far from the banks of the Ganges, in the midst of a garden full of roses, he entertained us to tea. His venerable patriarchal appearance and eastern courtesy ran in curious double harness with his almost fierce nationalism. It was also interesting that this modern among Hindus could not let me into his exquisite and splendidly equipped library unless I removed my shoes.

No part of this Benares pilgrimage was more moving than walking round the precincts of Saranath. This place is as sacred to Buddhism as is the north end of the Lake of Galilee to Christians; for here the Buddha first made known his message to the world, and here is believed to be the deer park which gives to Buddhist art one of its loveliest symbols. It is deeply moving to walk among the excavated ruins and gaze at the colossal *stupa* now in process of restoration, and to stand under the shade of the sacred Bo tree, a grandchild of the tree under which Buddha received his enlightenment. From that original tree a cutting was planted in Ceylon, and the tree at Saranath was brought as a seedling and planted there. But the new Buddhist temple and pilgrim hostel, opened in 1932, would surely be nearer to the heart of the master himself. Buddhism, ruthlessly uprooted from the land of its birth so many centuries ago, is now being replanted there at Saranath. Curiously enough a German Buddhist is its guiding spirit, while many of the gifts toward the temple come from the present home of Buddhism in China, Japan, Burma, and Ceylon. The pilgrim hostel was given by a rich Hindu. The monks of this new growth meditate and worship here at Saranath, where the founder of their faith taught, and then go out, as did his disciples, as missionaries of the Way. Nor can their teaching be without effect on the new generation if many of them have the zest, the fresh outlook, and eagerness of the young Indian monk with saffron robe and shaven head who talked to us of their ideals as we walked over those sacred fields.

As we entered the temple with unshod feet he expounded the story of the Buddha as reproduced in the vigorous and characteristic mural frescoes which occupied years of the energy of a young Japanese artist. The immortal Buddhist art of the Ajanta caves had obviously, either directly or indirectly, controlled his handling of both the figures and of the detail, especially jewellery.

The little school of depressed class children under a tree, where one of the boys, under the teacher's guidance, was expounding to the others the arithmetic on the blackboard, and a dispensary for sick folk, are first-fruits of the new emphasis on social service which the redemptive work of Christianity has brought into the Orient.

We walked through the pleasant mango garden given by the government to an interview with Anagarika Govinda, the German Buddhist monk who has, as a goal, however distant, the creation in Saranath of an international centre of Buddhist teaching and missionary expansion. We were asked to take off our shoes before entering his cell, and there sat cross-legged with him in discussion. With characteristic German thoroughness he had come to Buddhism through prolonged examination of the faiths of the world. As he was telling me this, my gaze, wandering above his head, caught the lettering of H. G. Wells's *Outline of History.* A little book by Brother Govinda, *Art and Meditation,* just published, is illustrated with drawings in which cubes, triangles, and geometrical curves express pure emotion in line. He rejects the notion either that this is symbolism or intellectualism. He told me that, sitting on the deck of a primitive sailing ship in the Mediterranean he had shown one after another to a group of ignorant Sicilian fishermen, asking what each picture meant to them. As they looked at it, infallibly the men responded with a gesture and a word expressing perhaps perplexity or release, precisely the moods that had given birth to the drawings which in his book are called 'Labyrinth' and 'Liberation'.

The pilgrim who on reaching Benares had received a severe shock to his idealism had, as the reader will have seen, come through a bewildering range of experiences, from the Dom diseased criminal to the bursting vitality of the Hindu University, from the deification of nationalism to the pursuit of the Way of Enlightenment, from the hydra-headed polytheism of traditional Hinduism to the withdrawn sunlit peace of the Buddhist 'Perfumed Court Temple', and from the proud remoteness of the fakir and the Brahmin to the healing hand of the followers of the Good Shepherd.

There is only one fool in India whose crass stupidity is beyond forgiveness, and this is the man who seeks in some easy generalization a synthesis of forces which, as they reshape the destinies of her great peoples, burst the pigeon-holes of logic and only reveal themselves to the patience and the love whose ultimate fruit is wisdom.

CHAPTER VII

The Bengal Cauldron

MR. WORDSWORTH of the *Statesman* was rushing me along from the stately offices of that great Calcutta newspaper by the Maidan to the United Services Club when suddenly the driver jammed on the brakes and the car stopped with a jerk. I looked out and there lay two brown bodies, smeared in ash and wearing only a loin-cloth, prostrate in the road in front of the car. They doubled themselves up into a shape like that of the praying mantis insect and then stretched out again. They were Hindu pilgrims under a vow to travel to the Ganges, measuring their length every step of the way. 'They may have come', said Mr. Wordsworth, 'a hundred miles like that.' It was the week of the great Kali festival, the almost orgiastic Christmas of Hindu Bengal. By the time the pilgrims had crossed the wide boulevard scores of cars on either side had been halted. These men were so obedient to the discipline of their faith as to be apparently completely oblivious of the hurrying traffic of a twentieth-century city which they were dislocating.

Our car rushed on again, but as it swung along the road it passed a strange vision in a rickshaw. When the car reached the club I waited for that rickshaw and was able to photograph a well-to-do bourgeois Calcutta merchant holding in his lap the blazingly coloured pig-tailed image of India's most blood-thirsty goddess, Kali. Just before midnight the previous evening I had been led down a narrow street where hundreds of craftsmen were busily at work painting in scarlet and green and other colours the thousands of images of Kali that they had shaped during the previous weeks—Kali standing on her prostrate husband with gouts of blood dripping from her snarling mouth, with garlands of skulls round her neck, and corpses hanging from her ears. In ten thousand homes that week puja was done before these images, in which the people, as educated Hindus repeatedly urged upon me, worshipped not the image itself but the total process of creation symbolized in her demonic energy related to her husband's spiritual nature. Even the rather scientifically minded taxi-driver who took me under his friendly guidance, and who had had some education at Rabindranath Tagore's university at Santiniketan, was one of a group of taxi-men who had hired a room in which to place their own image of Kali for this celebration. It recalled to me the many thousands of Nativity cribs with the shepherds, the wise men, and the cattle made in uncounted homes and churches of Christendom. But what a difference in the imagery and the object of adoration! During the festival the streets blazed with ten thousand lights from every window and shop and roof-top. A few days later I saw bullock-bandies crowded with gaily dressed families carrying their Kali images, and multitudes walking, all going, as the last act of the festival, to cast the image into the water so that it should float away and melt on the breast of Mother Ganges.

Mr. Wordsworth led me into the spacious, cool, pillared halls of the club, where judges and barristers, district magistrates and colonels, prominent British merchants, members of the Legislative Council, and leaders in the professions gather together. My host was as genial a cynosure to the Indian scene as a man could hope to meet. A brilliant leader in the educational world, he had escaped from Government service to find the freedom of expression impossible in a State department. He is so deeply comprehending of Indian aspirations as to come under the sharp criticism of imperialist friends, yet is disciplined by the realism that no experienced journalist can escape. Again and again I came back to him during my stay in Calcutta to test the perspective built up in my mind by the fantastically varied experiences of that time. During those days I passed from the inner sanctum of Sir John Anderson, the Governor of Bengal, to be the only European in the Congress meeting which sounded the first blast of the electioneering trumpet aiming to bring down in ruin the walls of his governmental Jericho. Men who had been under detention for years as terrorists and other ex-prisoners like Mr. Sarat Bose, as well as Dr. Roy, doctor to the Nehru family and to Gandhi, opened their minds with great frankness, while an International Fellowship meeting presented a kaleidoscope of contradiction. From a long and happy interview with Rabindranath Tagore I passed, as already mentioned, to the young group of intellectuals in Calcutta who are known by the title of their monthly periodical, *Parachiya.* I passed from the Agricultural Camp, where scores of the young détenus charged with terrorism were at work, to the office of the Muslim Minister of Education, the Hon. Khan Bahadur M. Azizal Haque, and came face to face with the young student life of Serampore College, gathered from all over India, and the men and women of St. Paul's College and the Scottish Churches' College, whose experience goes back beyond all government institutions to the founding of modern Indian education by Alexander Duff.

I went to Government House to see Sir John Anderson with almost painful interest. Before leaving England talks with Indian friends, discussions with civil servants, and even occasional mild scenes in the House of Commons had quickened in me the conviction that India had no tougher problem to set before statesmen than the revolutionary movement in Bengal. I was, as we shall see, to come away with that conviction sharply quickened and intensified.

One's instinct of fair play and pride in the tradition that British processes of justice are available for all the subjects of the Empire made one more than uneasy at the knowledge that over a thousand young men in Bengal were, if not imprisoned, yet under definite restraint up to even periods of six years without trial. Would examination of the problem on the spot intensify or allay those disturbing qualms? The reason why these détenus, as they are called, are under police control lies in the 'terrorist' movement gaining its resources by dacoity (armed robber bands) and through which many officials, one after another, mainly in Bengal, were shot. Isolated assassination, under whatever provocation, is a loathsome thing; a sustained organized movement, drawing on an almost inexhaustible reservoir of unemployed young graduates with nerves exasperated by the febrile atmosphere peculiar to Bengal, is obviously a thing which statesmanship must grapple decisively with or else abdicate.

The use of the bomb and the pistol for political assassination in Bengal sprang from a number of contributory causes. Calcutta University has for long produced graduates in law and political history far in excess of the effective economic demand. The seed sown by British apostles of political freedom, such as Mill, Burke, and the rest, grew to tropical luxuriance in the over-abundant leisure of the unemployed intellectual. One of the détenus pointed out to me the lesson of the execution of Charles I as applied to Indian politics. A study of political agitation in the comparatively recent history of Russia, Italy, and Ireland provided lively western object-lessons in terrorism. Garrett and Thompson, in their book *The Rise and Fulfilment of British Rule in India*, point out that the statistics of assassination in Bengal were never, in proportion to the population, so high as in its heyday in Ireland. Edward Thompson has pointed out what he calls 'the low emotional flash-point of the Bengali'. The passions aroused in Gandhi's non-co-operation campaign of 1921 were held back from expression in violence by his teaching of *ahimsa* and his public repentance and fast when his doctrine of non-violence was transgressed. But with so much explosive young life about, murder somewhere or other was inevitable. Bengal has an historic reputation as the home of secret societies, so these began to develop among youth when Lord Curzon decided to partition the province in 1905, and waves of terrorism spread over the country at intervals. When Gandhi's promised early attainment of home rule by non-violent methods was seen to be a mirage, and he himself was imprisoned, a revolutionary society again became active. The secret police of Bengal, as well as of the central government of India, working in university and many other circles, assembled evidence of the association of thousands of young men and of some young women with this terrorist movement. Why, then, was this mass of accused youth not tried by ordinary methods?

With this question in my mind I approached Sir John Anderson. I went down the corridors of that regal Government House which Lord Curzon on his arrival found to be modelled exactly on Kedleston. Sir John Anderson's well-knit figure and dark, strongly moulded face give a first impression of almost saturnine strength until lit up by a gleam of humour or his friendly smile. He showed to me with great frankness the dilemma of the administrator responsible for the lives of his officers, while intensely anxious to administer perfectly impartial justice in a field where all evidence is under the gravest suspicion and where the terrorist's revolver would be as swiftly drawn against the witness as it had been against the official. To carry through the ordinary machinery of official inquiry in thousands of cases in these conditions would be at once farcical and futile, he said. His own method of safeguarding justice had been to call at intervals for the relevant files containing the police evidence and to pick out as many as he could possibly find time to grapple with, and this procedure completely satisfied the Governor that in the overwhelming majority of cases the men in detention were in closest complicity with the terrorist movement and that the investigations had been fairly conducted. One reason why the administration of justice in the British sense has been impossible is that, as Sir John Anderson puts it, 'our law rests on the assumption that the country as a whole is behind it', which is clearly not the case in contemporary Bengal.

My own mind after this interview was completely convinced of Sir John Anderson's own conviction of the justice of the method employed. The doubt that haunted and still haunts me is linked up with the gravest suspicion of evidence collected by police in a land where every Indian will admit that personal grudges are frequently worked off with vamped-up evidence against an enemy, and where the lower grades of the police are liable to corruption and false witness. It may be asserted that no other method of securing evidence was available. Even if that were admitted, it does not create confidence in the authenticity of the result. Such processes inevitably create the violence of reaction that government is trying to quell. It carries us indeed to the very heart of the Bengal problem. The police mind and police repression never ultimately settle issues that have powerful subterranean origins in psychology and economic need.

The fact that Sir John Anderson has risen above the police mind and introduced a dynamic ameliorative element above the static repressive one makes his administration of Bengal the beginning of a new era. I must confess to being more than startled by getting evidence of this not so much from himself as from men who had themselves been détenus.

I left the governmental palace to plunge into the heart of the Indian business section of Calcutta and found on a corner of Cornwallis Street the commercial museum. There in his tiny office I discovered the creator of that museum, Mr. Nyogi, who had been detained for three years in a camp as a terrorist. For a number of years before he was arrested Mr. Nyogi had been lecturing on the progressive decline of India's economic condition. A man with a vigorous and rebellious mop of dark hair and the face of a fervid orator, Mr. Nyogi, with the burning intensity of his convictions, is evidently a man to swing audiences to his will. He found a major cause of India's economic suffering, of course, in the selfish policy of the British Government, and I can well believe that his speeches would leave students seething with wrath. His gifts as a lecturer are suggested by the fact that for nine months 'Pussyfoot' Johnson took him through the United States as a lecturer on temperance. 'Terrorism', he declared, 'has subsided to the greatest extent. Terrorists are no longer lionized by the public in Bengal and get no public support. Old slogans such as 'Terrorism is bad, but slavery is worse' have now died down. We must', he went on, 'give Sir John Anderson credit for having thought of developing in the detention camps some real efficiency for livelihood when released. The fact that men are not only trained for either agricultural or industrial life under Sir John Anderson's scheme but are equipped with capital sufficient to launch out on their liberation, and still further have a market already secured for their products for some years ahead—the return of the capital being also secured on those sales—is a great step from punitive and revengeful to redemptive justice.'

This did not mean that Mr. Nyogi acquiesces in the process of holding men in detention or subjecting them to restrictions of movement, being forbidden, for example, to leave the house after sunset, and all without even telling them under what charges they are being punished. 'Detention without trial, the suspension of the Habeas Corpus Act,' he said, 'is un-British.' When I asked him what course he would take to try men, he said he would place both the government's case and that of the youth or his guardian before eminent, trustworthy judges, reinforced, if necessary, by public men of great experience and high integrity. 'Every man held in detention with his case unexamined and his parents' or his own position unstated is a fomenting centre of discontent. The neighbours see the mother weeping, the smaller children of the family are infected by an anti-government complex, the newspapers are gagged, and so discontent smoulders and spreads under the surface.'

What made my own heart leap out to Mr. Nyogi was that he was the first intensely nationalist Indian whom I had met who was urgently pressing, working, and planning to develop the village and civic industries of India without waiting to throw Britain out before starting. He sees India and England as sister sources of economic strength, as free and equal allies. He is out to harness rivers, exploit forests, stimulate village industries, fight malaria, illiteracy, and filth, and by co-operative enterprise lift from the bent shoulders of the peasant his titanic indebtedness. I went through his commercial museum that extends round three sides of a large courtyard. It is a vigorous and practical piece of propaganda in this direction. He has assembled fabrics, oils, metals, woodwork, indeed every sort of product of India's own hand or machine craftsmanship, and sustains a continuous propaganda to stimulate to ever-increasing degrees this industrial progress. He loathes the pride of the clerical graduate who will not lay his hands to a practical piece of work. That pride, he says, is a virtuous word for inefficiency.

He went off with the air of a Father Christmas to a Kali festival party where they were giving a feast to slum children, while I moved on to attend a Congress meeting. Seated on the platform surrounded by men, most of whom had been in prison for seditious speeches, I could not help wondering whether the owners of the curious eyes that were obviously bent on me in that crowded meeting thought of me as a new convert to Indian nationalism or as holding a watching brief for the Government. Most of the faces in that audience were those of men in the early thirties. Dr. Roy, the Nehru-Gandhi physician, was in the chair, from which he made the point, not agreeable by any means to every one, that acceptance of election and even of office under the new Constitution does not involve giving up the project of complete freedom.

All the speeches were in Bengali. It was an odd experience, in a torrent of words that were completely incomprehensible to me, to have phrases of English break out that clearly had no equivalent in Bengali. Among these I recall 'capitalistic mentality', 'British imperialism', and 'constructive work'. Notable phrases in Bengali that were translated for me by a neighbour included 'We will fight to remove all lawless law'; 'We are a nation without nationality'; 'The British Government has killed our nationality'; 'The taxes of the British are lashes on the backs of the peasant'.

It is rare that any man has made on me so powerful an impression of having every faculty instantaneously under complete command as did Dr. Roy. With a very large medical practice and the responsibilities of a member of the Senate of Calcutta University and of the Medical Association, a hard worker in municipal affairs, having been Mayor of Calcutta, and founder and helper in two hospitals and a medical college, Dr. Roy, who is a bachelor, found time to give me individual attention during a long interview, closely packed with challenge and penetrating analysis. 'Jawaharlal Nehru', he said, 'asks us to create more wants, industrialize and socialize the nation, and to organize a new India. Gandhi, on the other hand, tolerating as well as lamenting the evils of industrialization, calls on the people to go back to simplicity. That simple India will get strength to win freedom.' Dr. Roy's own conviction is that the present need of India is not, as he puts it, 'to discover how far we can compete in mass production with Britain or Japan, but how far we can supply our own needs. Until we can control our own tariff and exchange policies, no large industries can flourish.' This Dr. Roy regards as congruous with Gandhi's own vision. Gandhi says 'that in this materialistic world the less are your wants the greater will be the control of your mind over your body. This self-control is the basis of progress: the only way to realize our destiny.' Dr. Roy then gave me fascinating examples of the extraordinary control of Mr. Gandhi's own mind over his body. 'Two or three years ago,' said Dr. Roy, 'Gandhi was ill and down to ninety-three pounds in weight. He was eating then only six dates, with three or four oranges and six or seven almonds a day, with a little salt. I suggested that he should take some *chapatis*. He said, "No, wait a bit. If in a few days I don't add two pounds to my weight I will do as you say." In seven days he had added two pounds, which must have been fully the weight of his solid diet. I was with him during his twenty-one days' fast', Dr. Roy continued, 'and was amazed at the elasticity of his body, for I examined his blood every day. His uniqueness lies in the fact that he is an ordinary man who by dint of discipline and self-control masters himself. If he says, "I will sleep for two hours", in three minutes he is asleep and he sleeps for two hours.' This led Dr. Roy to another contrast between the two great leaders. 'Gandhi feels that if you can control yourself you can control politics. Jawaharlal Nehru thinks that the only way to control destiny is to drive away those imperialistic forces now in control. Gandhi says create an atmosphere that will itself destroy imperialism; Nehru goes out to destroy the system.' I asked Dr. Roy in what direction he felt the younger generation were going. He lamented that in the clamour of communal antagonisms so many were aiming at the loaves and fishes. It was a question of 'What post can I get?'

I raised the question with him whether, if you increase the economic strength of India and reduce mortality, you won't immediately have the pressure of increased population, again pushing people over the margin of subsistence. He countered this by the assertion that the land in India can deal with any population for a long time to come, given better agricultural marketing and consequent increased purchasing power. I raised the question whether reduction of the birth-rate is likely. He said that the original Hindu *shastras* laid down definite lines of marriage relationship evidently designed to control birth in a natural way, but, he added, 'the large bulk of people do not follow their teaching'. He said that the Indian view would be that artificial control is not for the good of the nation.

Happy is the ruler who, having initiated a new policy, discovers a man with both the enthusiasm and technical ability to carry it into effective action. Mr. B. L. Mitter, who drove out into the country with me to examine an agricultural colony of détenus on the new ameliorative model, is just such a gift from India to Sir John Anderson's policy. Mr. Mitter, who is a science graduate of London University, has revealed in his massive book, *A Recovery Plan for Bengal*,[1] the splendid talent for seeing the broad perspective of economic planning and its concrete application in detail to the complicated technical demands of every industry in Bengal. Drawing on the lessons of Moscow, Washington, the Economic Department of the League of Nations, Italy, and China, Mr. Mitter in that book has developed a scheme to which I know no parallel for scientific thoroughness and practicable project. When, therefore, Sir John Anderson launched his scheme in the early autumn of 1935, instead of leaving the matter to a department or a commission, he shouldered Mr. Mitter with the responsibility, gave him all possible facilities, and told him to go ahead. By handing the project to an Indian leader, giving him entire confidence and sustained backing, the Governor of Bengal has achieved the double result of getting the thing carried through with astonishing speed to unanticipated success, and in winning the hearts of multitudes of enthusiastic patriots. Industrial training-centres opened in Gourijore and Sukchur and an agricultural one at Maslandpur resulted in men being trained and equipped for industrial and agricultural activity more swiftly than any expert had believed to be possible.

As I tramped over the fields of the Agricultural Colony and watched the young men in their pith helmets and khaki shorts sowing, ploughing, and opening and closing channels of irrigation in a way that showed both enthusiasm and skill, it was easy to see that a great

[1] The Book Company, College Square, Calcutta.

psychological change had been worked. Young fellows who had been vainly seeking vacant seats in a government office or a precarious stool in a commercial firm and who, being foiled, had turned rancid, were now masters of the world's basic industry. The training that I watched them getting equips them not just to work on the land, but to direct the life of a small farm and control the labour of others.

One odd example, at once humorous and tragic, of the police mind emerged as I came to the attitude of the détenus themselves to the scheme. The young men's letters from camp to their relatives and others were censored, the principle of censorship being that they must only contain matters of domestic or personal interest. Repeatedly in the letters the men had broken out into praise of the camp and its methods and of the effects on themselves. These passages were blacked out by the police as not being 'of domestic or personal interest', although, of course, actually superb propaganda for the government.

Realizing that a man who has been under the shadow of government criminal law is terribly handicapped in securing work, the scheme now provides to groups of four or eight ex-détenus, as they pass out from the training, loans sufficient to provide land, plant, premises, and even working capital, and has gone further and helped to secure in advance the marketing of the goods produced. Out of that marketing, interest on capital and its ultimate repayment is secured. A small technical staff, under the Ministry of Agriculture and Industries, is helping the ex-détenus in both agriculture and in industry. I came away from the Agricultural Camp and went to an Industrial Centre, where youths were all busy making, for instance, very attractive walking-sticks and umbrellas from bamboo, for which there is a large market with considerable profit.

The success of the scheme, as I saw it, is really due to the fact that the Governor has given one man a free hand and full backing, and that that man, burning with altruism and intimately knowing the intricacies of Indian agriculture and industry, is inventively planning and driving ahead from dawn to dark. The actual work in its dimensions is, against the background of India, infinitesimal. Yet the more I look at it the more I am convinced that if Sir John Anderson's successors and men in other parts of India will take the cue and build up on this model a scheme of reconstruction, it will one day be seen to be a great step in the constructive revolution, for this principle of financing small schemes of agriculture and industry by credit, combined with a system of technical training and skilled guidance, all integrated first into provincial and then into India-wide planning, strikes at the root of India's present ills.

Neither the Governor nor Mr. Mitter, however, could have done anything had not a psychological change taken place inside the young men themselves. If we seek the source of that change, does it not lie in their recognition of a change in the purpose of the ruler? It was, to go back to the expression of that ex-détenu Mr. Nyogi, the change from the repressive and revengeful to the redemptive.

CHAPTER VIII

Gateway of East and West

'THE British mentality is the same as Hitler's. In their own estimation they are the superior race born to govern. Only those who successfully show fight get what they want from Britain. She always interferes on the side of reaction, and the League of Nations itself is just another link in the chain of bondage, for the *status quo* clause would fetter India for ever as Britain's subject.'

The passionate stream of denunciation flowed on. The story of Egypt and of India was ransacked to show why India could have no belief in British pledges. 'In politics as in economics this nation of shopkeepers always bargains; they never concede anything without first asking what they will get. No great man has any good word to say of the British politically'; and Sun Yat-sen, Kemal Ataturk, Count Keyserling, and Napoleon were brought into the witness-box against the British.

The speaker was an ex-mayor of Bombay opening a discussion in a group of us called together over a week-end to analyse the relations of Britain and India. Racially Indian, Parsi, American, British and one Anglo-Indian, and religiously Hindu, Christian, Parsi, Theosophist and free-thinker, we sat round for two days and discussed in a country house outside Bombay, most of us cross-legged upon the floor. The ex-mayor and some of the other Indian men wore the sad-coloured, long, high-necked coat made from *khaddar* cloth and the *khaddar* cap which mark the follower of Congress. The young Indian women, who took part freely and without self-consciousness in the discussion, looked delicately lovely in their saris of blue and rose and brick-red, mostly made of *khaddar* hand-woven from home-spun cotton. One of them, fiercely nationalist, with alternating moods of restless brooding and flashing smiles, changed her clothes as well as her moods. At times, with her boyish figure in long trousers and a blouse and her bobbed wavy hair, she looked like the very spirit of modern girlhood in the West. An hour or two later she would be draped in the graceful folds of a sari, which seemed to accord oddly with her rebellious hair and dark, burning eyes.

Between meetings we wandered in twos and threes through the beautiful garden of this country bungalow. Under the starlit sky we climbed a spiral staircase to the roof. As we gazed across the dark countryside to the lights of Bombay, the plaintive notes of Indian music rose from a portable gramophone. The tensions created by our discussions relaxed as the notes rose and fell like drops from a fountain of silver water, and the rising moon shed her light. The voices of argument were stilled and the little group on the roof from East and West drew together in simple friendship.

'Comradeship and co-operation will come', the speaker went on, 'when political and economic equality are achieved. So long as there are victimization and exploitation no progress is possible.' 'To talk of co-operation', as another one put it, 'between master and slave, superior and inferior, is hypocrisy. For India with Britain dominating her,' he continued, 'only three choices are open, and only one of these is possible.

There is acquiescence, or one can show fight—which is impossible as we are disarmed—so Gandhi's non-violent non-co-operation was a shrewd capitalization of a necessity. For the first time the Indian is able to respect himself. And we cannot work for the social and economic improvement of India till Britain's strangle-hold is taken off.'

The hammer-blows went on and on and on. The Muslim-Hindu conflict, which was at the moment working murder every night in Bombay itself, was, we were told, entirely the work of the British Machiavellian machination. The impoverishment of the peasant was the product of two processes of the British Empire: the levying of taxes and the juggling of currencies and tariffs in order to enrich the industrial magnate. The economic regulation of India's life was controlled by the London Chamber of Commerce for the sole benefit of Britain. Even when Britain surrenders her rule over others, as in the case of Iraq, it is simply because it was an economic liability. Britain, we were told, in past centuries found a peaceful, united, virile India, and had seized, divided, emasculated, and exploited the country.

For weeks on end I had heard practically every day in different parts of India one or other of these charges made against Britain. Here they came in battalions, but I had got leagues beyond being hurt or angry with those which seemed unjust. Years before I had suffered remorse for the share of guilt which is certainly on our shoulders. What did fill me with a dull aching despair was, first, the blend of real grievance with fantastically and demonstrably false history, whether remote or recent. How could we clarify issues in such an atmosphere where no objective assessment was possible? Secondly, there was no glimmer of a suggestion, or even an admission under challenge, that there were failings or faults on the Indian side. Communal conflict, for instance, however much the new constitution might accentuate it, was as old as the Mogul empire. But most baffling and maddening of all was the angry padding round in a vicious circle like a tormented wild animal at bay. As one of them said, 'Our subjection is a running sore and we can think of nothing else till we have got rid of it.'

In the intervals for meals and other forms of social intercourse East and West were on terms of happiest companionship without tension or forced demonstrations of friendliness. Indeed, there was a hunger for such fellowship as becomes natural on a basis of equality. Some of us of the West were the guests of this preponderantly Indian group. This very fact, of course, points the difficult way to a co-operative future for India. If but once we could get to the point where Britain is content to accept the place of guest and not conqueror, the transformation would have been achieved.

Meanwhile, however, the deadlock in our discussions, as in the situation, was unbroken. From the Western angle we were invited to make our position clear. We are, it was suggested from the Western side, at a stage of historic development. We have to do with the historic present. Leaving aside all question of truth or error, what is the value of constant denunciation of the British mentality? It does not alter by an iota the realistic position. At the moment we have a Government in Britain which is the direct product of a unique world situation. The situation and the government will pass; we are in a state of flux. Can we not then co-operate to work out the next step and take it —we people of goodwill who accept the challenge of equality of status as a goal?

On the first evening I went to my camp-bed on the roof, glad of the calming influence of the stars above me. For the circle of impossibles seemed to be unbroken. In the morning the opening of our discussion brought new elements into the field of thought. The speaker was an eminent young Indian lawyer who began by telling us of his three years of happy natural contacts with the British as a student at Oxford, but on returning to India he found them to be impossible. 'India is a caste-ridden country', he said. 'The English have fallen victims to the poison in the atmosphere. We tried to break the circle by the Phoenix Club which existed for inter-racial contacts, and Europeans and Indians dined together. But the race feeling was too strong. One Englishman even had to leave his business house because of his insistence on keeping social contacts with Indians. I came to look on the British as despots over my nation and they on me as an enemy of the Empire. The Indian in dealing with the English becomes either a toady or abusive.'

The speaker then analysed contrasted types of imperialism and nationalism, which was a great help in clarifying the atmosphere. 'There is', he said, 'the imperialist with a sense of duty who honestly feels that Britain is here for the benefit of India, and who is neither petty nor mercenary. Lord Curzon was of this type. The other is out to exploit the Indian markets for England, sees the country simply as a field for a career, is mundane and mercenary, and believes in the right of the sword to prevail. Similarly, there are two absolutely contradictory nationalisms. One is aggressive and violent, and desires domination—the European type of to-day; the other, like the Indian, is non-aggressive and non-violent, wanting only freedom and unity within the nation. This nationalism in India simply wants to teach the Parsi, the Hindu, the Muslim, and the Christian to think and act together as Indians. If India got her freedom, the bonds between Britain and India would be stronger. These bonds are in fields of language, literature, in world strategy and commerce. India when she is free cannot stay isolated in the world, and Britain is her natural ally. What we want in Britain is a man of the calibre, courage and spirit of Campbell-Bannerman.' What was in his mind, of course, was the unique act by which when the Boers had at last been conquered in South Africa, the new constitution put through by Campbell-Bannerman gave them entire equality in every respect with the British, so that in point of fact South Africa has been under Boer Prime Ministers ever since. The most brilliant of Britain's enemies in the Boer war, General Smuts, became one of the half-dozen greatest personal forces in the empire in the Great War.

The Indian speaker lamented how India's most brilliant sons like Nehru are doomed to carry on a fighting attack when they are longing to do constructive work. 'We cannot bend our energies to solve India's social problem until this political problem is solved. Social reform is always carried through by minorities, and with the British Government in power it is bound to be neutral; where it leans it leans to the majority.' This speaker believed that the new constitution must be worked and not just sandbagged. To the end, however, his view was a minority one in the group discussion. The more numerous were the more radical, and they claimed to represent the multitudes of young men in India who feel that their time and money and blood in prison were wasted in Gandhi's non-co-operation campaign. Disillusioned, their conviction is hardening into something both politically and economically revolutionary, and the feeling that their end can only be achieved by force. From the American War of Liberation, from Ireland to Egypt, examples were cited to show that Britain never gives freedom till the sanctions of force drive her to it. I ventured to point out that there were no voices in America so eloquent for her colonists and her freedom as were those raised in the British House of Commons by Burke and Pitt, that British generals had surrendered their commissions rather than fight against the colonists, and that European mercenaries had to be hired as fighting forces. Similarly in Egypt and Ireland, from Gladstone onward, the most potent allies of liberation were within Britain herself. I recalled the great saying of Gladstone when Palmerston inveighed against the project of the Suez Canal as a peril to our rule in India: 'I am unwilling to set up the Indian empire of Great Britain in opposition to the general interests of mankind.'

As the talks drew to a close I envisaged more realistically than before the danger that the despair of Young India might, under some new leader who had been drinking in both the Communist and Fascist doctrines of force, precipitate a revolution, and I realized how stupendous a task rests on the shoulders of Nehru and his colleagues, for in that bloodshed, if it should come, the suffering would be inflicted principally, as always, on the peasant and the adolescent youth.

My experience in India, of which this group conference was a focal point, has strengthened to certainty the conviction which has been upon me for years now that this problem of human relations in India is one on which world history may well swing. If the League of Nations has for the time failed in its central task of 'the peaceful settlement of disputes', the peaceful settlement of this Indian dispute, affecting a sixth of the human race, would change the psychological climate of the world. To the achievement of that most difficult task the putting aside of cherished grievances and preconceived notions is one necessary step. To the total task of conciliation and comity every man and woman of goodwill in the English-speaking world is called.

Sometimes, as one talks either with Indians or with British on this question, one feels almost stifled in a jungle of misunderstanding. Progress is only possible as a path is cleared through the jungle—as the Englishman recognizes that India belongs to the Indians and must in all things be governed for their benefit; as the Indian recognizes how much of what he characterizes as deliberate malice is due to lack of imaginative perception on the Englishman's part; and as each by an act of will opens his mind to the truth and gives value to the contribution of the other, both actual and potential, to an India in which the gifts of each shall have made a home for all.

Within three hours we were plunged into one of India's most hideous social problems, whose solution is delayed by these political tensions. The girl with the short hair and the brooding eyes took us for a tour of the Bombay chawls. By day she teaches in a school for her livelihood; her spare time is given to the service of the dwellers in this area of slums, worse than anything which can be seen in any big city in the West. Under one roof, a large family to one room, are gathered hundreds of municipal or mill-workers, some in one-story buildings, others in tenements of two or three stories. As we approached the first compound, we saw lights flaring and were greeted by shrill clamour and noise—the hum of a great multitude of Indians in conversation; below it the rhythmic beat of drums, above it boys' voices singing Indian lyrics. On the dusty, beaten earth of the courtyard hundreds of people sat cross-legged in long rows. Before each was a leaf-plate on which had been placed little heaps of food and a leaf-cup of water. The occasion was an inter-caste dinner, when sympathetic caste folk, casting aside the inherited prejudices of centuries, eat ceremonially with sweepers, who by the nature of their unsavoury task of dealing with sanitation and refuse are considered to be unclean. That there shall be no mistake about the genuineness of the gesture, the food is cooked on the spot by sweeper women, whom we saw busy at their fires in a little enclosure. The food is of the same coarse variety as that to which the sweeper is accustomed, but is luxury compared with the scraps of food from the refuse heap on which he often has to live. Each guest at these 'love-feasts' pays for his own meal.

A somewhat cynical friend to whom we described this experience suggested that the inter-dining was more spectacular than actual, because the elections were near, when the support of these despised but numerous sweepers was evidently desired by the Hindus, as in a system of communal representation their ranks would be swelled against the Muslims. We did not see whether a large number of caste people were present, but those who were there, seated cross-legged on the dusty ground among the sweepers, certainly ate the food prepared by the hands of out-caste women.

Leaving behind the heat and dust and din, we passed on to the chawls. Only the pen of a Dante could do justice to their suffocating, stench-ridden atmosphere, to the acrid, smoky, stifling heat of each little room, to the apathetic faces of the women and the heart-rending listlessness of their heavy-eyed babies. We stumbled along the dark alleyways, thankful that it was the dry season, for in the rains, our guide told us, they would be open drains. My heart was in my mouth at every step after I had nearly walked on a naked babe who had fallen asleep with his head pillowed on the dusty earth so near in colour to his own brown skin. We shuddered as we remembered stories of the rats which infest these dens of misery.

We asked permission to enter some of the tiny over-crowded rooms, which held the whole life of a family. The heart was most wrung with compassion in those where pathetic attempts had been made to give a home-like, cheerful atmosphere, where the few possessions were neatly arranged on shelves and a few highly coloured cheap lithographs were tacked to the smoke-blackened walls. In the villages from which these people came, they would have lived in a one-room hovel, but most of their days would have been spent outside the hut in the open air and cleansing sunshine. There would have been, too, a measure of privacy, each family able to live its own life without being perpetually overlooked. Some of the chawl rooms are provided with a slip of a kitchen to hold the open fire used for cooking. In others, where there is no such provision, we saw the women crouching over their cooking-fires built in the covered alley-way just outside the door. The eyes smarted and the throat burned in the acrid reek from the dung-cake fires which hung like a dense pall in the long, dark corridors. One tried to imagine what it would be like to live there always in that foetid atmosphere.

At some considerable distance were the latrines, in sickening juxtaposition to the water-tap which served each chawl community.

A survey made in 1936 of the chawls for municipal workers in Bombay showed that of 1,138 rooms investigated, 227 rooms were occupied by more than three adults and children, a total of 1,053 persons being found in them. In 31 of these minute rooms the average number of children per room exceeded five. The case for the investigator is complicated by the strong family loyalty of the group. Brothers and sisters, uncles and cousins come to the city to look for work; lodgings are expensive. What more natural than that the family established in the chawl should take them into the already over-crowded one room? So the investigators found, for instance, in one room two couples, five children, a widowed mother and another adult; in another one couple with their four sons and their wives; in another three couples and five children; while one couple with two children, one widowed sister with three children, and a widowed mother occupied another. The Conservancy branch of the Bombay municipality employs over 3,100 workers, most of them as scavengers. Men employees pay a rent of 8 annas per month and women 5 annas. Those living in the chawls who are not in municipal employment are required to pay rent of 2 rupees for a man and 1 rupee for a woman.

Efforts are now being made to improve housing conditions in both the municipal and mill-chawls, but progress is slow. Often opposition comes from the people themselves, as in the matter of overcrowding. When tenements are built with sufficient provision for fresh air, tenants are found who stuff the windows with gunny-bags, in many cases probably to obtain a measure of privacy for the women of the household.

The death-rate per 1,000 for the whole of Bombay has been reduced in ten years from 270 to 220; in the chawls, of course, it is deplorably higher. There is little chance of further reducing the mortality rate because 75 per cent of the whole population of that great city live in single-room tenements. But diseases formerly rife are now being held in check; plague, cholera, and hookworm have been eliminated. All water-cisterns are now closed, and there is a weekly examination of every tin of standing water to eliminate the mosquito. In this respect conditions are a vast improvement on those in the outcaste villages from which the workers come, where in many cases the only water-supply is a stagnant pond, in which the people wash themselves and their garments before taking from it the water used for drinking and cooking. In North Bombay there are still some open drains with consequent malaria, but measures are being taken which it is hoped will eliminate this disease also within the next five years. The schools committee has the power to compel children to attend school, but in a floating population from the country it is very difficult to carry education through to a satisfactory stage. Gradually, as the matter is taken more seriously, the number of children not attending school is reduced.

The public conscience in regard to this open sore has quickened during the last two years. I was interested to find when making inquiries about the chawls from the responsible municipal officer that he directed me to the wife of a professor in a missionary college as the first expert in Bombay on the subject. With the growth of the socialist ideas in Congress other bodies feel that they must help to improve the lot of the poor. Voluntary bodies investigate the facts and bring pressure to bear on the municipality and on the mill-owners. The International Labour Office presses labour legislation. The conditions under which these poor folk live wring the heart, but the outlook is brighter now than it has ever been.

In the drawing-room of my host and hostess in Bombay I awaited the coming of a young man who was of the extreme Socialist wing of Congress. It came over me as I waited there in the house of Principal and Mrs. Mackenzie of Wilson College, one of the leading centres of Christian education in India, that here at least was one place where the extreme rebel and the Government officer, the Hindu and the Muslim, the Brahmin and the outcaste, were all made to feel genuinely at home. This was one of very few houses in Bombay of which this would be true. I felt it was due to the confidence placed in the unassailable integrity and catholic sympathies of Dr. and Mrs. Mackenzie by all sorts and conditions of men and women.

As I talked with the young Indian Socialist leader, I felt confident that some bitter personal suffering lay behind his uncompromising rebellion against imperialist and capitalist control of life. Yet his sense of humour broke through. 'It is really funny,' he said, 'that the British Government tracks me down as a Communist while the Communists curse me for refusing to open the door of the Congress Socialist Party to them so that they may capture it.' As I read afterwards the manifesto of this Socialist Party I could well understand the difficulty any one might feel in distinguishing clearly between its explicitly Marxian ideology and the Communist creed. As the statement of the Party, adopted in 1936, says, 'The Party's own programme must be a Marxist one. . . . Marxism alone can guide the anti-imperialist forces to their ultimate destiny. Party members must, therefore, fully understand the technique of revolution, the theory and practice of the class struggle, the nature of the state, and the processes leading to the socialist society.'

If left-wing socialism were growing only among the urban population it might, in an agricultural land like India, have relatively little importance. An entirely different aspect, however, is put upon the situation when we realize that it is spreading among the peasants. Peasant socialist societies developed by the All-India Congress Socialist Party are getting an increasing hold on the rural population, as many as thirty thousand being enrolled in Bihar alone.

It was one of the many transitions of this Indian

experience to pass straight on to the sanctum of Lord Brabourne, then Governor of Bombay Presidency. It was distinctly entertaining to find that both he and his aides cherished humorous wrath against me for punishments they had suffered at Eton for inadequate study of a book that I wrote years ago on the race problem.

In repeated talks with Lord Brabourne the poignancy came over me of the situation of a man desiring intensely to penetrate to the inner heart of the life for whose government he is responsible, yet, by the very fact that every act of a Governor is a public act and that all his movements are organized in advance, unable to overleap the barriers between himself and that informal intercourse without *arrière pensée* through which alone truth can be apprehended. He candidly and earnestly expressed envy of the opportunities open in such a pilgrimage as mine for full and frank talk with all and sundry. As my mind went back to the accusations of malignancy and cynical despotism hurled against the British rule by Indian colleagues in the group discussion already reported, a double need revealed itself—first, a far greater personal intercourse between those holding clashing views so that there be less beating the air, and, secondly, some humanizing of the overwhelming bureaucratic machine of our overseas governmental system. How many times in India has the statue of the Laocoon wrestling with the entwining serpents come into my mind as I have watched humane and freedom-loving officials writhing in the entwining tangles of miles of red-tape!

In the desire to get a judicial balanced view of the total situation I sought out an eminent lawyer respected throughout the length and breadth of India for his balanced judgement, Mr. M. R. Jayaker. I put questions to him as to what are the trends he sees in all departments of Indian life, what are the things happening in the social life of India to-day, in its economic and political ideas, its religious reactions, its cultural development, which were not there say five years ago. He was so intrigued by the problem that he asked for time to get his ideas sorted out during a day or two of travel to and from a centre where he was to advise a group of leaders of various Indian States as to their policy with regard to coming into the federation under the new constitution.

Before we launched into an analysis of Indian trends we enjoyed a little gossip about the university at which we had both studied. I found that when I was an undergraduate there he was, as he put it, 'knocking in vain at the doors of Balliol', which the Master, Dr. Edward Caird, whom the young Jayaker had regarded as 'very crotchety,' refused to open. 'We already have six Indians in Oxford', said Dr. Caird!

Dealing first with the trends towards social reform, Mr. Jayaker described this as the great need of India. 'The Indian wants command of government,' he declared, 'in order to put forward social and religious reform, and in order to improve the lot of the poor.' Congress, he predicted, will split into two sections, which he described as the stagnants and the progressives. 'I look forward', he said, 'to a long, perhaps twenty-year, period of social reform. In the stress of that battle other distinctions, like the Muslim and Hindu tension, will disappear. We shall turn from our zest in beating the government with anything we can lay our hands on to working out the grounds of social, economic, and political reconstruction. In that fight Jawaharlal and myself will be on the same side. The Englishman', he went on, 'cannot possibly deal with social reform. He lacks the knowledge of Indian conditions, and because of the principle of neutrality, he lacks the courage to act. Nor does he know, as the Indian does, what value to attach to opposition. For instance,' said Mr. Jayaker, 'Gandhi's temple entry bill was not supported by the government because of the factitious, fictitious opposition—so because the government was neutral, a great and needful reform was put on the shelf. I regard the disintegration of the joint family life coming in India to-day as more hopeful. In the old system you had the father and perhaps six sons with all their wives and children, and an illiterate mother-in-law ruling the roost; now you have young graduate wives who refuse to play second fiddle under the domination of an ignorant mother-in-law. The old order was a wonderful scheme of life and had great values, but it is going and cannot be revived.'

Discussing the trend of the labour movement, Mr. Jayaker was full of hope. 'My peon', he said, pointing to his servant who was waiting to take a message, 'knows all the latest currents in politics. The best educated people are leading labour and working for its freedom and organization. In Bombay there are six or seven daily papers with tiny sheets at a *pie* a copy, selling some 30,000 to 40,000 in an edition, and being read by working people in the buses and the trains and at home.'

'Up till recently,' he continued, 'the mechanistic materialism that has been brought in by the ruling race has tended increasingly to dominate us. Now, however, as the importance of the rulers is diminishing, we shall discriminate. As a passport to social standing it has been the fashion to imitate the West. That is beginning to pass. We shall sift things and accept or reject them on their merits. To take an example: the knife, fork, and spoon in place of the fingers will remain; they are embedded in Indian life. Exotic things that are unsuited to the country will disappear. We have reverenced with blind adoration all that the West taught; then in rebellion and political reaction we have tended to detest it. Now the third process of discrimination begins.'

In religion Mr. Jayaker is a liberal Hindu, and holds that the main teaching of Hinduism is to adopt in your own life all of which you approve in other religions. 'In your life,' he added, 'not in your faith. All that is great and glorious in the world is from the divine. What you do saves you and not what you believe.'

I came away feeling the glow of Mr. Jayaker's idealism, and wishing that his predictions of progress may prove to be true prophecies. I could not, however, repress questions as to their realism, and I wondered how long it was since Mr. Jayaker had walked through the half-starved India of the depressed class villages, whose total population is twice that of Great Britain, or the villages of the small farmers of the middle castes, where a population about equal to that of the United States has never used a knife or fork, and where the joint family system has hardly suffered the smallest fissure. I wondered whether he had been into Travancore where, following the legal establishment of freedom for the outcaste to enter the temple, orthodox caste Hindus had left those temples as being desecrated.

Nor can I see in the vast lethargic multitude, wedded to immemorial custom, the driving force for 'twenty years of social reform'.

Looking back over the total experience of Bombay I felt that tumbling of contradiction upon contradiction that defies prophecy or even generalization—the over-articulate orators and lawyers, with, to the western mind, a defective sense of the realities of the historic present; the governmental mind desiring ordered well-being within that existing framework whose foundations are already crumbling; the dumb suffering masses whose real preoccupation is not with the Government of their country nor with mystical contemplation, but with the problem of where the next meal is coming from.

CHAPTER IX

Seats of the Mighty

'I AM tired of this India of ferment and political strife', said a friend. 'I want to get away from these tensions and problems. The India that I really want to see is the India of the Taj Mahal, Akbar's deserted city of Fatepur Sikri, the Great Mosque at Delhi, and some of the ancient temples.'

As one whose life is largely given to trying to get a world perspective of the nationalist, racial, and economic turmoil of to-day, I too hail with joy the chance of turning one's back on the unrest, of recovering poise and finding that release from tension which saturation in beauty brings. And when that beauty rises in an exquisite majesty built by the hands of man centuries ago, the long and lovely perspective steadies the spirit.

So we looked at the beauty of the Taj Mahal as the setting sun threw its quiet softening light on the superb dome and minarets whose white marble gives too hard and brittle a reflection at midday. When darkness had fallen and the white building faintly glimmered in the starlight, it was like a creamy lotus floating on the dark waters of the night. Down below the terrace the last boatman punted his craft across the broad waters of the Jumna. The heat of India's conflict rolled back and the calm of the centuries flowed in, as the coolness above these cypress-lined waters that throw back the last reflections of the Taj conquered the heat of another Indian day. Overhead the swift, intent flight of birds, seen black against the glimmering marble, seemed like the passing of time across the face of eternity.

Before dawn we were again hammering at the outer gates and from one angle after another watched the light of the new day reveal the exquisite detail of the workmanship in which romantic married love has found its lasting memorial.

Along the road used by Akbar, the great-grandfather of the Emperor Shah Jehan, builder of the Taj, we travelled the twenty-three miles from Agra to that unique long-deserted royal city of Fatepur Sikri. It is a city that throws the visitor with any historical imagination into a strange excitement. For here, within the encircling walls of seven miles circumference, is an Indian Mogul city of Queen Elizabeth's time in the condition in which Akbar left it when he returned to Agra after a few years owing to the impossibility of getting good water, and because of the surrounding malaria. FitzGerald's Omar Khayyam came back irresistibly during the hours spent roaming and resting there:

> They say the lion and the lizard keep
> The courts where Jam-shed gloried and drank deep.

One had the impression that that lost world had suddenly come alive again as we passed into the courtyard of the mosque within that deserted city. It buzzed with the gay chatter of a holiday crowd of Muslims on the eve of the Feast of Id. The ancient white-bearded guardian of the mosque derives his position from descent from the saint who, foretelling the longed-for birth of Akbar's first son, gave Akbar his incentive for building the new city. Exquisite as is the beauty of the mosque, what overwhelmed me was the blended majesty and loveliness of the Gate of Victory. I was intrigued by the aged guardian's translation of the famous inscription which is inside the gate:

> Jesus, peace upon him, said,
> The world a bridge, walk across,
> Do not make a house.

Because of the story surrounding the birth of Akbar's son, this mosque is a favourite resort of women desiring a child.

To circle round the country outside Delhi and visit one after another of the buildings put up in those great Mogul days was to get a glimpse of that astonishing renaissance born of the marriage of the virility of warriors from the highlands to the culture of Persia.

The shock of the contrast between New Delhi and the capital of the Moguls challenges us to form a judgement on the colossal city that we have built during this century. I felt its unquestioned beauty to be cold and impersonal as contrasted with the Gargantuan domesticity of Akbar's city. That is possibly the natural and inevitable expression of our titanic bureaucracy. Along the miles of corridors of the New Delhi government offices peons in scarlet dress move to and fro with dun-coloured files tucked under their arms. New Delhi represents the greatest revolution that has come imperceptibly over Indian government—the transition from the personal rule of the old type of civil servant who moved slowly round in camp and gave judgement under a tree to the impersonal régime of a man anchored to his desk, scribbling on file after file responses to requests for 'your necessary obs.'. Where Government does come into first-hand touch with the Indian to-day it is mostly through Indian officials, whether district magistrates or school inspectors or the police.

With the drastic criticism of Indian leaders ringing in my ears, I was anxious to get some glimpse from within of the government at work. I was only able to present my introduction to H.E. the Viceroy at the moment when his travelling kit was being carried out for his Christmas stay in Calcutta and subsequent tour in Burma. But I was able to get guidance from his private secretary as to the men who would best give help from the angle of government on my quest for trends in Indian life to-day. Armed with his recommendations and with other introductions from friends in England, I walked the corridors of the Secretariat seeking the heads of departments who could enlighten me on economic and rural as well as psychological movements in India.

In a man like Dr. John Mattai, who brings first-class economic technical training and a penetrating progressive mind to the whole-hearted service of his country, I found just that blend of authentic knowledge with a humane standard of values and a true perspective that I sought. He confirmed by direct evidence my sense of the growing place of economic matters in the public controversies and governmental programme of India. The Legislative Assembly proceedings are a clear index of the predominance of this economic trend. Even the vehement political agitation among village people from 1930 onwards was greatly stimulated by the fall in the price of foodstuffs. The fact that the cost of manufactured goods had fallen less squeezed the peasant still further. He showed how this stiffens the movement towards class-consciousness and class-war. Three things are happening simultaneously. First, a new capitalism has been growing up in India alongside an ever-increasing multitude of officials who, with their relatively high salaries, form a kind of new official aristocracy, and the interests of both groups align them with the existing feudal landlordism. Secondly, at that moment the income, already meagre, of the hundreds of millions of Indian peasants grew less. At the same time —and here is the crux of the situation—political power under the new constitution is diffused among the peasants who are feeling angrily their economic inequality. This puts a great weapon into the hands of the left wing leader of Congress. He has simply to develop among the newly enfranchized the conviction that the underdog has no economic chance in present conditions, but that he has some political power and could make good use of it. In such a situation, as I myself have discovered in different parts of India, politicians are making fantastic promises that cannot possibly be redeemed. It is often argued that once they are in power in government they will be found out, but such a desperate situation is just as likely to drive towards more furious revolutionary activity.

My own conviction that there are vast areas of India where something like Communist revolution may come to a head within the next decade was strengthened by this objective evidence. The situation, as I have seen it, amounts to this. The peasant, through the fall of agricultural prices and the reduction of markets, is very much poorer, and unnumbered millions are tottering on the edge of the precipice of starvation. In an area like Bengal (and it is not unique) the great landlords are absentees, living often opulently in city mansions. Between these feudal zemindars and their starving tenants stand hordes of middlemen as rent-collectors and so on, who remorselessly squeeze the peasant. Helpless, he raises money from the money-lender at often exorbitant usurial rates, pledging not only himself but his children's future. He is thus doubly a serf, and to him comes the government tax-collector. Has there ever been anybody in the world of whom the ringing message of the Communist manifesto is truer—'You have nothing to lose but your chains'?

Suddenly for the first time this peasant becomes, from the fact that he has a vote under the new constitution, the object of the affectionate solicitude of the astute revolutionary politician. Of economics in the abstract sense he knows nothing, but stories come to him of how the peasant in Russia has wiped out the landlord and a revolution has made the worker the dictator. Could there be more fertile soil for a no-rent campaign? It only awaits some such catastrophe as the preoccupation of Britain with a world war demanding every soldier to defend other frontiers, coupled with the emergence of an Indian Lenin, to precipitate tremendous upheavals with incalculable consequences. Indeed, even without a catastrophe such as we have envisaged, this volcano might erupt.

No conviction about India is stronger in my mind than the urgent need at the very centre to have an organization that relates every branch of the economic life of the sub-continent, and that sets out to enlist Indian public opinion to see how that life can be reorganized. Palliatives applied here and there and all conceived within the framework of the existing economy are mere pills to fend off an earthquake. The presentation of economic matters so far in the Legislative Assembly seems to reflect an economic outlook that most governments surrendered some thirty years ago. The Viceroy's encouragement of agricultural revival may well be the focal point around which economic planning for India could be developed. Mr. L. B. Mitter's economic planning for Bengal, already described, is an eminent example of provincial initiative.

I could not help wondering whether it was a mere accident that the outstanding realistic economist, Dr. John Mattai, who received me in his office in the Secretariat, comes of the oldest Christian stock in India. An as eminent English economist in India, with whom I had long personal talks, expressed it, 'Righteous indignation in the defence of the under-dog has no basis in Hinduism. It cannot have. *Karma* goes deep down into conviction of fate: what I am and am suffering is something that I have deserved. This is true of the poorest of the outcastes. We are', he pursued, 'in danger of relying in India on an infiltration of the Christian ethic into Hinduism without the ultimate Christian dynamic. I believe similarly that in its anti-religious drive Communism, which owes its impulse to the teaching of Jesus, is cutting off the branch on which it sits.'

Another outstanding government official pleaded strongly for an extension of the newer government policy of going out to meet India's problems and meeting them in advance instead of waiting for a conflagration and then putting it out by repression. As an example to set alongside Sir John Anderson's dealing with terrorism in Bengal by agricultural and industrial training, he quoted the effort of Lord Brabourne in Bombay to reclaim criminal tribes (such as those we saw in Benares) by developing employment.

It was a great relief to have the benefit of checking

my variegated and often contradictory impressions with Mr. Ian Stephens, the Director of Information. His most moving contribution to my thought was to realize that population is fundamental to the whole Indian problem. If a solution could be found to this, he felt it would revolutionize the entire situation. Every ten years now India is adding to her numbers more than the total population of France. The population of India, as the Public Health Commissioner himself has estimated publicly, will be over four hundred million at the next census. These new mouths to feed are always more than overtaking any increased production of crops.

We called, with an introduction, on one of the six members of the Viceroy's Executive Council, whose standing is like that of Cabinet Ministers in England, and whose official residences, each in a beautiful spacious garden, stand in a quiet corner of New Delhi. Sir Muhammad Zafrullah Khan, who received us graciously, has a strong face, with iron-grey hair and a fringe of beard. He was dressed in western clothes. The time was just after four o'clock on the last day of Ramadan, the great Muslim fast, when from sunrise to sunset for a lunar month no food, not even a drop of water, must pass the lips of the good Mussulman. Before we could come to the object of our visit, the member excused himself to say prayers in the little mosque which stands in the garden. He is a member of the Ahmadiya sect.

'I lead the prayers,' he explained, 'but when I am not there my chauffeur leads them. If I go in late and he is taking them, he just carries on . . . I will order some tea for you in the drawing-room, but you will have to excuse me from taking any for it is not yet sunset.' He led us to the huge drawing-room, tastefully furnished in western style, with a Persian carpet which made us draw our breath. Then, putting on a red fez, he strolled across the garden to the mosque. While we were drinking tea and feeling very greedy because our host had eaten nothing all day, the conversation turned, as always at some point it does turn in India, to politics. 'As a member of the government', I suggested, 'perhaps you can help us on this point. Often it is said to us that the policy of the Government of India is really directed by the London Chamber of Commerce and that the welfare of Britain rather than of India is the goal in commercial and industrial affairs.'

Sir Zafrullah warmly denied this, and gave several instances, for example one purchase of railway locomotives where preference had not been given to Britain. 'Price', he said, 'is the only consideration. Germany put in a lower tender; Germany got the contract. On another occasion, however, I was criticized for giving an order to Britain instead of to a firm in India, but the British tender was cheaper—that was the only reason.'

He reminded us that the next day would be the Muslim Feast of Id, which marks the end of the month's Fast of Ramadan. As soon as the new moon appears the Fast is over, and the people rejoice. The festivities take somewhat the form of the English Christmas with special food and greeting cards. There is an Id holiday, and after morning prayers the Muslims go to each other's houses to carry their greetings and enjoy the day together. The member suggested that we should go to the great mosque in Delhi next morning to watch the prayers from above the gateway; and also invited us to an Id tea-party at one of the big hotels. As the setting sun was suffusing the sky with golden light, our host walked with us through his garden. In the middle, leading from one part of the house, was a portion railed in by a brick wall of open trellis work. 'That', he said with a smile, 'is for the ladies of my household. Do you think they are so badly off in purdah?' We moved through the garden gate on to a great stretch of park land in the heart of New Delhi, with a vista of two miles of green grass, trees, and ornamental water, and a sudden glimpse of two flying figures—a man and a woman—galloping along a replica of Rotten Row. We looked back to that purdah garden.

Next morning at nine we set out for the mosque, and joined the crowd going up the outer steps. At the gateway Muslims removed their shoes. We Europeans were provided with unsightly canvas overshoes, so that the dusty leather of our shoes should not contaminate the holy place. Up winding stairs we were taken to a balcony in the gateway from which we looked across the enormous courtyard to the mosque itself. In the centre of the courtyard was a large oblong marble tank sunk in the floor. Two erections at each end like diving stages gave it the look of a bathing-pool. As the worshippers came in they went to the tank, stooped and performed their ceremonial lustration.

Long before we arrived the mosque was crowded to the doors, but an irresistible flood of worshippers continued to pour through the gates into the courtyard. They took up their places in long rows on the matting which the mosque authorities had laid down on the floor. Men, women, and children were all in their most colourful clothes. As we looked on them from above, the courtyard was like a moving flower garden. The murmur of thousands of voices filled the air like the humming of bees on a summer day, punctuated by the shrill voices of children as they played unchecked around the family groups. The morning had been grey and rather cold, but now the sun broke through the mist, giving added colour to the scene. We watched a little group just below us. The father and two boys wore long tight-fitting silk damask coats in brilliant pink, red, and puce, with tight trousers in daringly contrasted shades. Father was crowned with a magnificent canary-yellow turban; the boys wore small round caps. Mother, crouched on the ground, was a symphony in royal blue, emerald green, and purple. The dainty little daughter of about five years old, obviously the spoiled darling of the family, teased her brothers by taking off their caps and replacing them at rakish angles. Then she ran roguishly away and stood in gleeful expectation of being pursued. A quaint little creature she looked, like a humming bird in her immensely full long skirt of scarlet with bands of silver embroidery, under which her tiny peacock-blue slippers played hide and seek. Her head and shoulders were swathed in an emerald green gauzy cloth bordered with silver, which she adjusted with a grown-up practised movement whenever it slipped as she ran about.

Nearly 10.15. The crowds were denser than ever, surging through the gate at the last moment. The thunder of a gun reverberated through the clear air. It was the signal for the prayers to begin. A sudden hush fell on the assembly, the quiet made more intense by the crying of a baby here and there or a young child's sudden laughter. Late-comers hurried to the tank to purify themselves.

The *imams* (leaders) stood stiffly to attention in those erections which looked to us so much like diving stages. The people rose to their feet and stood in long tightly-packed rows. We felt almost suffocated by the intense expectancy of the moment. Then, taking their time from those within the mosque, the *imams* led the prayers. With the precision of military drill the people followed them with disciplined swaying movements. Three times that vast crowd sank to their knees and bowed with their foreheads to the ground. It was as if a sudden wind had blown over a golden cornfield starred with poppies and cornflowers, bowing the slender stalks with one magnificent gesture. Each member of the great congregation must have been acutely conscious of his solidarity with all the others; they rose and fell as one man, class and sex distinctions wiped out for the time, humble worshippers before Allah, the All-Merciful, the Omnipotent. The gaily coloured groups stood erect again. Suddenly, as if at an inaudible word of command, they bowed from the knees. As they rose, with arms raised, a long-drawn triumphant shout rent the air—'Al-lah', 'Al-lah'. Three times they bowed, three times the challenge of their faith rang out.

The tension slackened, the *imams* descended statelily from their platforms. The crowd, moving towards the gates, began to laugh, to clamour, to call shrilly from one group to another. Prayers were over—and now for the fun of the fair! As we walked among the crowds outside and watched them buying sweets and other sticky delights, crowding into the little entertainment booths, gazing at three tired and dusty elephants in an enclosure, reading the sandwich board decorated with tinsel that announced the latest films, we felt that human nature is akin all over the world. The good temper, the joyous abandon of the crowd reminded us of London holiday-makers on Hampstead Heath. Two features, however, were different. Sitting on the mosque steps or mingling with the crowd were beggars in revolting rags, many of them displaying sickening deformities or loathsome sores. Abject, impudent, suffering, indifferent, truculent, they thrust grimy hands towards us, pouring out streams of cajolery and threats, the only word which we recognized being *backsheesh, backsheesh*. Allah the Compassionate had been worshipped inside the mosque; we wondered how many of the worshippers had felt impelled to relieve the suffering of these poor wretches. Mahomed, their Prophet, had not said 'Forasmuch as ye do it unto the least of these my little ones, ye do it unto Me'. And when we arrived back our host asked anxiously, 'There was no disturbance, I hope?' No, we were able to assure him that everything had gone off quietly; there had been no Hindu demonstration. For on religious occasions, either of the Muslims or the Hindus, there is the fear of communal disturbances, and the prayers have at times ended in ugly scenes of riot and bloodshed.

CHAPTER X

The Face of Mother India

I BUMPED over four miles of rough track from Wardha towards the village in which Mr. Gandhi lives. It is, as he put it recently in a letter to a friend, 'a proper village', that is, without a post office or a store for the sale of foodstuffs, and with no access to medical aid. A central part of his aim in living there is to be cheek by jowl with the outcaste where the outcaste is denied access to the public well and suffers his normal disabilities under Hinduism. To Gandhi this village symbolizes the whole situation and, true to himself, he desires to live his principles out concretely on however local a scale.

Coming into the sunlit courtyard, with two well-fed cows and a few goats to provide the Gandhi household with its daily supply of milk, I went towards the single-roomed cottage where he lives. Built with mud walls its tiled roof comes down far enough to shade the raised mud veranda which runs round three sides of the building. Gandhi came out to greet us with a warm welcoming smile. Standing erect and vigorous there on his veranda he startled me with the impression that he was taller and less emaciated than when I saw him in London some years ago. The chills of a London autumn may have made him cower within his wraps, while here he expanded in the warmth of the sun. The oblong room, dimly lighted by two small unglazed windows and two open doorways, was arranged so that he sits in one corner, on his right a low wall nearly two feet high with a flat top. On the other side of this wall, close to the door, sits his secretary, Mr. Mahadeo Desai, with his note-book, ready either to take down letters from dictation or a record of conversations with visitors. This has been found important for two reasons; first, because so many writers and speakers have made public statements or published articles and books which Gandhi complains are inaccurate, and second, because a considerable part of his weekly periodical, *Harijan*, is made up of records of these interviews. The report, for example, of my own interview with him ran over two issues of *Harijan*.

On the veranda, engaged in his Islamic prayers, was a tall Pathan, Khan Abdul Gaffar Khan, who has been called the Gandhi of the North-West Frontier. With his daughter he is living with the Gandhis, as the British Government does not allow him to be within reach of the Frontier. A long talk on the veranda with Abdul Gaffar Khan was sandwiched between two interviews with Gandhi himself. Famous as the creator of the Red Shirts on the North-West Frontier, he has been regarded ignorantly as the creator of a wild revolutionary movement with 'Red' tendencies. I am certain that nothing in the world is further from being his aim. The garment called the 'Red Shirt' is of a rather dull brick colour, which happened to be the cheapest dye available. The actual title which he gave from the beginning to his organization is Khudai Khidmatgar, which, being interpreted, is Servant of God. Every person joining this movement, which he started in October 1929, has to take this oath: 'I regard all men, be they Christians, Hindus, Parsis, Sikhs, &c., whoever they may be as God's creatures, and I am their servant.' They were to be against all tyranny, whether of the Muslim, the Hindu, or the Englishman. The movement spread like wildfire and within a few months had drawn in forty thousand volunteers. What Abdul Gaffar Khan really wants is, on the one hand, to free India of the British Government and on the other to pacify the North-West Frontier by education with a spiritual foundation.

His greatest hero, one might almost say his *guru*, is Dr. Wigram, who years ago, as headmaster in a Church Missionary Society high school, taught him as a boy. He speaks of him with loving enthusiasm, and in his public speeches has again and again talked of the sacrifice of the young man in giving up the enjoyments of London to come out without salary to serve the Indian people. Two or three sentences from the speech made by Abdul Gaffar Khan for which he was imprisoned will illustrate the *naïveté* of his attitude, combining as it does religious fervour with political dynamite. 'I want you to realize that Christ came into this world. The Government then in power used to oppress the poor very much. Christ came in order to release them from the clutches of the tyrants. Moses came for the same purpose. The first thing he said to Pharaoh was "Liberate all the Israelites who are enslaved". Our movement is a religious and social movement. We are based on non-violence. The Government said, "If you organize the Pathan community you may use it against the British rule."'

Having in mind the fiery character and the ignorance of the Pathans of the North-West Frontier it is quite clear that the Government's fear of what might happen would not be without foundation; but talks with some of those who went out to round up Red-Shirt groups showed me that the task aroused in them a sense of distaste for the job and pity for the victims. It is difficult to avoid feeling once more that a more direct approach, with less reliance on reports made by police spies suffering from the inevitable mentality of their occupation, could have led to a more human dealing with the problem. This, instead of producing exasperation and a smouldering sense of injustice, would have pruned the movement of its dangerous elements. I can well believe, however, that it was impossible to let the movement run its course without some governmental action. If captured by some leader who, unlike Gaffar Khan, was ready to use force, a movement that had drawn in so many highly inflammable people could have produced an explosion. Gaffar Khan is himself not only a disciple of Gandhi but, unlike Nehru, is thoroughly dedicated to the doctrine of *ahimsa* and non-violence. Yet there were passages in the speech for which he was imprisoned which Gandhi himself regarded as technically seditious. Gaffar Khan pressed on me with enthusiasm his conviction that if the British Government would provide him with the requisite funds for five years he could lay foundations for the pacification of the North-West Frontier by a system of village schools and dispensaries. Every morning at Segaon, Gandhi told me, Abdul Gaffar Khan takes part in a devotional reading and meditation, which combines Muhammadan, Hindu, and sometimes Christian elements.

I was deeply moved by the spirit of simple loving-kindness and gentle courtesy that flows so naturally from Mrs. Gandhi, for whom the depressed class workers of the village were building a tiny separate cottage in the courtyard. This will give her the privacy impossible in the existing accommodation of the one-roomed cottage which is always open to visitors and the veranda on which I talked with her as she did her spinning.

When I told Gandhi of my talk with his doctor as recorded elsewhere, and put to him the question whether he saw the Indian movement swinging from destructive to constructive revolution, he answered that the centre of the movement was shifting from the city to the village and that when the villagers realize their own power, when they get that consciousness, they will become irresistible without lifting a finger against anybody. 'That is why', he said, 'I have settled down in a village. It is a good type of village. For four months of the year it is surrounded not by water but by mud. It is therefore untouched by so-called civilization. It has some six hundred inhabitants of whom half are Harijans.' Gandhi always uses this word, meaning 'Offspring of God', to describe the depressed classes to bring whom within the fold of Hindu society has become his central task.

'The village people here are mostly utterly illiterate', he went on. 'Before coming here I had a meeting with them asking whether I might settle in their midst; but in reply to my question they could hold out no hope of giving the Harijans access to their caste well. The well from which I draw my water is not used even by the Harijans. When I invited the only scavenger to use the well which the Harijans have, they themselves were up in arms. A silent revolution, however, is already taking place. I am working to teach them to use their waste hours. When I do this I put several thousand rupees in their pockets.' And he went on to tell me how he secured for them the right to tap the date-palm and then to crystallize its sap into a kind of sugar for which there is a big demand. Gandhi's argument is the one so characteristic of him, that it is only by beginning with the individual and the small group right on the ground that men will become capable of self-support and self-control; and that in proportion as they do this their rise becomes irresistible. It is the argument which Booker Washington half a century ago worked out in relation to the parallel group in America of the ex-slave illiterate Negro.

In response to a question by me whether it is not necessary, in addition to training the Harijan, to fight his enemies, such as the usurious money-lender or the corrupt middle-man of the landlord, he replied: 'We do not need to fight the money-lender. He will make himself scarce when he is not wanted. He is now a much-wanted man.' So he came back to his point that when the people see the value of using their time in productive activity and acquire the skill to do it, their rise in power and freedom will be irresistible. 'When that happens', he asserted, 'the evils of the zemindar landlord and of imperialism are sterilized. They do not need to be taught by me the inevitability of class conflict.'

In this connexion I think of the film on rural reconstruction already referred to, which I saw in Bombay. In that film, which I was assured by the Indian professor who took me to it was, in the main, a true picture, the forces of reaction are represented by the priest, the money-lender, and the zemindar's agent, who exploit both the villagers and the zemindar. These, the villains of the piece, put up a strong resistance to the forces of progress which would destroy them. Ajoy, the hero, is seen at the death-bed of his friend, who has given up his career in the city to dedicate his life to the service of the villages. The dying youth is deeply distressed at the thought of leaving his work unfinished and Ajoy decides to devote his life to carrying it on. But Ajoy is deeply in love with Protima, a wealthy, gently nurtured girl, whose father has given his consent to their marriage. He cannot ask Protima to share the hardships of his life in a village; he must give her up. Her father is furious about what he deems to be the insult to his daughter and declares that he does not believe Ajoy's story. Protima persuades him to take her to the village from which Ajoy has written. She will prove to her father that Ajoy was telling the truth and to Ajoy that she too can face hardship in the service of her country.

Meantime in the village Ajoy is inspiring the peasants. Singing songs to the motherland they fill up the unhealthy pools of water which breed mosquitoes, they sweep and tidy the village, they begin to make a road. The money-lender, the priest, and the zemindar's agent try to undermine his influence. They whisper stories to his disadvantage, which some of the villagers believe. Collecting a crowd whom they have inflamed against Ajoy they advance threateningly and with insults on the joyous crowd of peasants who are making the new road. Just as a pitched battle is developing Protima arrives with her father in a bullock cart, in which they have driven many miles from the nearest station. She is just in time to throw herself in front of Ajoy and receive on her forehead the huge stone which had been intended to fell him.

During the time of Protima's convalescence her

enthusiasm for the work grows. When she is well again she takes her place at the head of the women. Exalted with an almost religious passion the procession of women sweeps through the village, singing songs to the motherland, waging war on flies and dirt and disease, co-operating with the men to make the village healthy and prosperous.

The reactionaries put their heads together. Ajoy and Protima have too big a following to be injured openly; they must harm them by stealth. The zemindar is induced to enter into the plot. He pretends sympathy with Ajoy's work and gives him a large donation. Immediately the conspirators notify the police of the loss of these notes. Ajoy is searched, the notes are found on him, and he is arrested. The villagers turn against Ajoy; he is a thief. There is a plot against Protima, too. She is persuaded into a promise to marry the zemindar —old, a widower, with a weak heart—believing that thus she can save Ajoy and get his innocence established. This is worth any sacrifice, although the girl shudders at the fate in store for her as the zemindar's wife. The agent, to prove his good intentions, contrives to get Ajoy released. In spite of Ajoy's heart-breaking sorrow and passionate protests, Protima insists on keeping her promise to marry the zemindar. She goes through with the ceremony, until, as the final vow is to be taken over the sacred fire, her courage fails her and she refuses to go on. The shock is too much for the zemindar's weak heart, and he collapses. Protima sends a messenger for Ajoy, who is a doctor. The zemindar, believing that he is dying, repents of the wrong he has done Ajoy and Protima. He has been a weak tool in the hands of his agent. Seeking to make amends, he bequeathes his whole property for the good of the villagers. Under the loving care of Ajoy and Protima his health begins to improve and his agent is terrified. Refusing to be defeated he kills the zemindar by mixing poison in his medicine and gets the lovers arrested for murder. But the chemist from whom the agent bought the poison saves them, and the fickle villagers rally to them again. Once more Ajoy and Protima take up their work.

In response to a question I put to Gandhi as to whether credit for movements of reform should not be given to the self-sacrificing labour of Christian missionaries and Indian Christians, he replied, 'I do believe that a reforming conscience has been stirred by missionary work. They have developed literacy, carried out industrial training, turned bad women into good nurses,' and then he went on to argue that now that Hinduism is reforming itself from within, the Christian missionary enterprise should cease from working to win the Indian depressed class peoples to their faith.

As I listened to Gandhi speaking thus, I could not help wishing that the efforts, so far in vain, to get him to witness if only a part of the spontaneous movements of the Harijans in so many areas to demand Christian teaching, and to see the extraordinary transformation that takes place in multitudes of groups and in individual lives, had been successful. I wished that he could hear his brother Indian, Azariah, Bishop of Dornakal, expressing his own experience within the area for which he is responsible. Bishop Azariah, himself of depressed class origin, with practically all Christian missionaries withdrawn, has seen 125,000 people within fifteen years come into the Church of their own momentum and after searching tests and sustained teaching. Nor is it possible that this can be for loaves and fishes, for there are none to give. More searching still, I would like Gandhi to cross-examine the tens of thousands of caste people who ever since 1930 have come asking for similar teaching, declaring that their reason is not any plea from Christian missionaries or even from Indian preachers but the new cleanliness, the self-respect, the greater honesty, in a word, the transformed lives of the outcastes. I may here say that I have been into this matter at first hand, from Travancore in the Madras Presidency, up through Dornakal into the great mass movement at Medak in Hyderabad State. If Gandhi would take a month of his busy life to examine realities at first hand, some mutual comprehension between himself and Indian leaders like the Bishop of Dornakal might result in the fruitful co-operation of powerful influences to uplift the peasant folk of India.

The gesture made by the Maharajah of Travancore on the advice of his Dewan, Sir C. P. Ramaswami Aiyer, of opening the gates of the temples to the Harijans, has been acclaimed far and wide as a great gesture of goodwill and enlightenment. Behind it lie two great facts. First, that between the last two censuses the Christian population of Travancore rose from a quarter to a third of the total population of Travancore, and that Christians in large numbers are buying land and becoming an increasing power in that still predominantly Hindu state. Secondly, in February 1936 in Quilon, in Travancore, an executive group of the Ezhava depressed class community numbering two millions voted in favour of their community leaving Hinduism, the decisive majority in favour of becoming Christians. The transfer of two million people to the Christian community would come near to turning Travancore, whose rulers are Hindu, into a state with the Christians preponderating in numbers and in influence because of their superior literacy. The opening of the temples is a gesture to them to turn their faces back toward Hinduism, which has up to this point held them in their depressed condition and even refused to recognize them as Hindu. A young group of rebels concentrated the argument into a vivid challenge, 'When the Hindu community gives sugar to the ant and milk to the snake but refuses a cup of cold water to the outcaste, turn your back on him for the hypocrite that he is.' It would seem as though this new attitude on the part of the state has been successful in arresting this mass movement, probably to the ultimate benefit of the Christian community. For those who now become Christian (and large numbers were being baptized during the weeks that I was in Travancore) obviously will be coming from purer motives and not in such masses as to overwhelm the teaching capacity of the Church.

Rabindranath Tagore was whole-heartedly engaged in rural reconstruction work long before Gandhi had turned from his civil disobedience campaigns to concentrate upon the peasants. 'I had my mind filled with this idea', the poet said to me, 'and was looking round for a colleague to help develop it. Mrs. William John Van Moody, to whom I mentioned my wish when she was here, mentioned Mr. Elmhurst, who was then in Cornell University studying. On writing to him I got a cable offering to come. I wrote that we could not offer payment, and he replied that not only did he not want money but that he would bring it to the scheme. He not only did so and helped to organize the unified rural life of our village, persuading the peasant youth to come into it, but he also showed our student boys the example of manual labour.' This, as all who know India will recognize, is a crucial and most difficult achievement in a land where the scholar or professional worker scorns to soil his hands. Mr. and Mrs. Elmhurst from England, whither they returned, have helped to provide nearly Rs. 50,000 for this work. The work now is supervised by Mr. G. D. Ghose, who is continually developing further the community life, basing each advance on a project arising from a concrete need. The boys' fire brigade, for example, developed from a village fire, and has been priceless from the point of view of discipline and drill. The need to fight malaria led to courses in zoology, drainage, and mapping. The congestion of the local fair led to development of community first aid and policing. Entomology has concentrated upon the insects that attack man and his plants: the mosquito, the caterpillar, the beetle, and so on; and entomology with botany works toward silk culture. Rotation of crops, the breeding of better poultry producing better eggs, the development of practical weaving, the institution of a village tannery, and work toward co-operative marketing are all elements in the constantly modified rural development at Sriniketan which lives like a sister colony alongside Santiniketan.

Looking across the whole of village India I see embattled against the depression of sixty or seventy million outcastes and the economic anaemia of over two hundred million low-caste farmers, a multitude of movements and agencies working for their uplift. From the Viceroy to Mr. Gandhi, from Dr. Hatch's leadership of the Y.M.C.A. rural reconstruction in the south to the village improvement movement fostered by Lord Brabourne in Bombay Presidency, with Dr. Heinrich's enterprise near Lahore and that of Sam Higginbottom already described at Allahabad, with Rabindranath Tagore's rural reconstruction work at Sriniketan and that of the Servants of India from their notable centres in Poona and Bombay as well as the Ram Krishna service and other movements of reformed Hinduism, a splendid array of forces are at work for the uplift of the peasant. Was not Dr. John Mattai at Delhi right when he told me that the outstanding need is for some central nerve-ganglion, a clearing-house where the best experiments of each can be pooled for the good of all, and the men and women who are disheartened at slow progress in local areas can take courage from a vision of the whole vast field?

Men, Indian and European, who throw themselves with enthusiasm into helping the depressed class peasant to grow richer crops from better seed, to breed more productive fowls, and to get out of debt to the money-lender, nevertheless throw up their hands in disgust again and again at the lethargy and resistance they encounter. If we could really discover and dissipate the causes of this experience, we should have in our hands a key to the transformation of India from weakness and subservience to power and freedom. For the development of lively initiative in the peasant, strengthening him with better food and healthy, clean living conditions and creating the radiant elasticity that comes from doing our work successfully alongside our fellows, would bring the nation irresistibly into the control of its own destinies. What then are the causes of this tragedy? How can India be purged of them?

One group of causes of the resistance to betterment lies in the psychology of the depressed. The peasant breaks out into a spasm of wild extravagance that will leave him in debt for years, it may be for life. For a day at his daughter's wedding the sweeper is a king dispensing favours. For a night while drunk on toddy he is in paradise. We see here the characteristic 'escape', the day-dreaming of the frustrated. The outcaste, again, resists, as all depressed groups in the world do, the rising of individuals or small groups above the general level. He rejects outside pressure even when it is for his good. Hence the back-biting, the subtle insults, the creation of obstacles—all those methods of tripping up the progressive—which bring balm to small souls imprisoned within their own inferiority. Scolding those who are extravagant, who drink, or who hamstring progress often simply intensifies the evil. It has been proved in practice that what does lift the outcaste is the new belief in himself that comes from being led into action that demonstrates to the world his power to achieve. When you and your ancestors have been told for millennia that you are worms it is not easy to become lion-hearted. Whatever our assessment of Gandhi's contribution to the world may have been or may still be, mankind in general and India in particular will remain in his debt for some priceless contributions in this field.

He has had the courage to act on convictions without seeing any force to back these beliefs except that he is sure that they are true. Professor A. S. Wadia, of the University of Mysore, goes so far as to say that 'by far the greatest service that he has rendered to India is that he has battled with fear and conquered it in himself and taught others to conquer it . . . in a country where the people have been paralysed through fear: fear of the police, fear of the military, fear of public opinion, fear of social ostracism, fear of ghosts, fear of shadows'.

Again he has wedded ethics to politics in face of the most arrogant attempts in the West and the Far East to enthrone the acts of the state above the moral law. He insists that power to effect results in the world of politics grows in the soil of one's own personality. 'To conquer the passions of the mind seems to me far more difficult than to conquer the world with arms.'

There is in Gandhi an incalculable quality which has repeatedly given him the air of a man of destiny. The waters of the slow surge of the mass mentality away from him are fed by a trend from belief in the power of ideas in themselves to a conviction that ultimately force must be used to make them prevail. Although Indians know that at present they do not possess the instruments of force by which they might wrest from Britain its rule over them, the conviction grows that Britain will never relax her grip until force is used or until India has the unity, the strength, and the will to compel Britain to yield what she will never freely give. This is in essence entirely different from Gandhi's doctrine of *ahimsa* or the power of the soul.

To make an entertaining catalogue of Gandhi's inconsistencies of word and deed is as easy as rolling off a log. He assails machinery as evil yet uses trains, cars, aeroplanes for his letters, printing-presses, and speaks into the microphone at Congress, and therefore by implication accepts the mills and factories where the machines are made. He assails doctors, but is rejoiced and grateful when they save his life. The inconsistencies are quite serious. They seem to me for the most part to reflect the fundamental unresolved conflict within himself between Hinduism, which is at root a religion of escape from the wheel of the illusion that the material order is real, and Christianity which affirms life and the material order, and sallies out to its redemptive conquest with spiritual forces. Convinced of the equal value of all men in the sight of the Eternal—which, by the way, has never been a tenet of Hinduism—Gandhi has in recent years thrown all his uncompromising energy into a battle to reform Hinduism from within so that it may be purged of the great crime of caste and of the outcaste.

The significance of Mahatma Gandhi in the historic process seems to me to overleap even the frontiers of the struggle for Swaraj. I see him as a counterpart to Hitler and Mussolini, Kemal Ataturk and Stalin: men making contradictory appeal to that vast hidden entity whose acts decide history—what Jung calls 'the collective unconscious in its racial or national mass' and what Gierke discusses as 'group personality'. When the chief in an American Indian tribe on some upper reaches of the Amazon sits controlling the drumming of his boys on the tribal tom-toms, and first by their quiet throbbing calls his men round him and then by an intensification and quickening of the drum-beats thrills and stings them into a collective ecstasy and in a final gesture drives them out on the war-path or the hunting foray; and, as the braves start back, greets them, and with a gradual softening of the drumming wins them back to the normal domestic work of the tribe, he has captured and mobilized the tribal collective unconscious to a supreme common end. In that state and act they are as one and act as one. Gierke's phrase 'group personality' does not seem to me to overstate the reality. What happens in a primitive tribe seems of relatively small moment in world history. When, however, at the head of a modern nation of untold potentiality a chief sits, and with the drums of the wireless, the press, mass-drill, mass-gesture, and the Swastika symbol (inverted, by the way, in the wrong direction) or the Fasces, he whips and stings that nation to frenzy, to an ecstasy of oneness, the very Muse of History must hold her breath. For if by a barbaric gesture that chief, that Hitler or Mussolini or Japanese war-lord, launches the nation whose collective unconscious he has wrought to an exaltation of ecstatic obedience upon the hunt and the fight, the whole world will be drenched in blood and the ultimate temporal catastrophe for mankind will be reached.

Some of the profoundest psychologists in the world to-day are, I understand, coming to the conviction that Man, as a corporate inheritor of the eternal values in our ordered civilization, can only sustain that treasure if his collective unconscious in its national or racial grouping can be fired and fused for beauty and truth and goodness by some such power as inflames it to barbaric goals. For it is quite clear that this racial unconscious soul has not only a desire but an urgent necessity to feel and to express enthusiasm. Indeed, kingship is a creation of that need.

If that is so, may it not be that Gandhi's supreme contribution is that he has adventured farther on that higher road than any man has ever done? His ideals of non-violence and soul-force go far back, at least as far back as the Cross. He adopted them after reading in prison the New Testament, Tolstoy, Ruskin, and Thoreau. When, for example, he launched on his famous salt-march he saw, by some psychological intuition amounting to genius, how to make a ritual dramatization that would exalt multitudes to ecstatic sacrifice. When Gandhi started on that march, even so intimate a friend and colleague as Jawaharlal Nehru was perplexed and more than doubtful of the idea and its outcome.[1] Then Nehru saw that, as the leader went afoot along the dusty ways in his loin-cloth day after day, two strange things happened. In the person of that frail man men saw India on a pilgrimage toward freedom—unarmed, without wealth—the incarnation of an idea and an ideal moving through sacrifice toward fulfilment. The fact that he moved day after day on that slow march followed by increasing multitudes gave the newspapers, first of India and then of the world, the chance to rivet the gaze of humanity on that strange man. So, when at long last he stood on the beach and committed his simple act of non-violent defiance of Britain, making salt and refusing the payment of the tax, India saw herself—and the world saw India—in a single fearless dramatic gesture defying the power of the greatest Empire that the world has seen. A new hour in Indian history opened. Many thousands of women broke from the sheltered seclusion of their homes and in exalted devotion suffered the lathi-blows of the police and the crude harshness of prison. India straightened its back, took new courage, caught a glimpse of itself as one; and felt ready to pay the price of freedom.

Later the movement sagged; much lethargy set in; and mixed motives in some leaders sapped the enthusiasm of the multitudes. In one sense, the present disillusioned attitude of youth is comprehensible. They

[1] See Nehru's *Autobiography*.

went to prison but the goal was not reached. Swaraj did not come. Yet the event remains historic, not only for India but for the world. The life of the women of India will never go back behind the curtain. India's own sense of what she can do when she is one in devotion to a great end has baptized her sons and daughters into a fresh consciousness of the power of dedication. Twice, in 1925 and 1931, Gandhi has shown the world that India's masses—her collective unconscious—can move with the sweep and power of a tidal wave. He has thus, in a certain way paralleling Hitler and Mussolini, effected some elements in the ritual needed to stir the collective unconscious: the *khaddar* raiment for the black or the brown shirt; the spinning-wheel for the Fasces or the Swastika; and the public advertised fast to force the hand of government by mass-emotion.

These acts of Gandhi are the experimental phases. Will another person come who will play the Lenin to Gandhi's Tolstoy? Will an Indian Stalin move that tidal wave to a full-flowing tide? Will it be possible to arouse that tidal movement of the collective unconscious to ideal rather than to low aims? Or will the new leader lurch back to barbaric ritual to achieve a gross and hateful goal?

The problem plunges too deeply into ultimates for me to try to grapple with all its implications here. I can hardly leave it, however, without asking—although unable to suggest an adequate answer—whether Jesus, seeing in the Kingdom of God that ideal end which is at once within man and yet is the goal of his pilgrimage, did not in his Temptation turn his back deliberately on precisely those lures to which the Hitlers and Mussolinis are succumbing. Again, when the multitudes thronged from all sides and a mass-movement surged forward to make him king, did he not with his eyes open to the consequences refuse to satisfy their political nationalism; and from that time many fell back from following him? It would seem as though Jesus refused to use any gesture or incitement to sting the collective unconscious into corporate action.

Has not Gandhi himself by harnessing the self-seeking of merchants to a kind of economic blockade of Britain and by—as Rabindranath Tagore put it—closing the windows of India, compromised with the barbaric forces? Was not even the non-violent, non-co-operation movement simply a recognition that against the armed force of Britain no physical fight was possible? The essential will-to-power simply took the only path available.

Jesus did, however, in a simple meal of a group of men around himself create the eternal symbol of his sustained presence in the corporate life of that world-body which is called the Church. Of that Body he is, so far as it opens its life to him—if we may dare to put it so—the collective unconscious; he is the soul of that group personality. And on the Cross we see him going through to ultimate sacrifice rather than compromise with the barbarisms of either imperialism in the person of Pilate or exclusive nationalism in that of Caiaphas. If this line of thought with regard to Christ follows, however remotely, the trail of some reality that eludes adequate expression in words, then his Body on earth could, if and when it should live his life and express his spirit, show to mankind the Kingdom of God on earth and call man to seek it.

CHAPTER XI

India of the Princes

SIR MIRZA ISMAIL, the Dewan or Prime Minister of the State of Mysore, governed by that enlightened Indian Prince the Maharaja, was going on a run through numerous villages and some small towns and invited me to go with him. To the right of him sat one of the principal executive officers of the state, and in front, by the driver, an officer in charge of seeing that the decisions of that day in that area were carried out.

Talks with the Dewan, and the sensitive solicitude of his hospitality, had shown me already that here was a man knowing intimately the politics of Europe and the Far East, holding in his hands the reins of great state affairs, and simultaneously having an amazingly swift eye for grasping detail and making instantaneous decisions. I found that I was to spend the day in incessant confirmation of these impressions.

'Have those trees dug up and palm-trees put in their place.'

'There is a bad dung-hill in that village—it must be removed.'

'Have that bad drain removed and an L-shaped drain put in its place.' . . .

So the instructions succeeded one another as we swept along. The Dewan has a passion for making his villages and roadsides at once beautiful and fruitful. He is a master of peasant psychology and every village has at each end of it two dignified granite pillars bearing the name of the village, on the one pillar in English, and on the other in the local language. He has proved that this simple device has had an unmistakable effect in giving the people a sense of responsibility for their village and a pride in it.

As we enter a large village a decorated archway becomes visible and on either side of it a group of men and women and children. The panchayat or leading group of the village in their best turbans come forward as the car stops. Garlands and limes are extended, and we get out of the car. A new stud bull, one of the many that the prime minister has introduced to improve the breed of the people's cattle, is tethered in the village square, as are a ram and a he-goat. Quickly we inspect the village school. There is a rapid fire of criticism by the Dewan of a defective porch, of a window darkened by unnecessary shutters, followed by appreciation and attentive listening to an appeal for a better water-supply for irrigating the fields. The officer responsible for the water-supply declares that he cannot improve it. 'Let them petition Allah', he says, 'for rain, not the Dewan.' He admits, however, that if at a certain point the channel of the river were deepened the people's needs could be met. Within two minutes with a quick to-and-fro argument between the villagers and the officer, the outlines of the problem are perfectly clear. The Dewan decides to have the channel deepened, dictates a couple of sentences to the officer with the notebook, the villagers cheer, and we go back to the car. From my experience in the War in a government office I could clearly visualize the eight or ten months during which files would have circulated back and forth, at last possibly to be pigeon-holed.

This was only one of at least a score of cases during

that single morning and early afternoon when I was impressed as never before with the positive benefits of wise and benevolent despotism. Farther on we inspected the large tobacco-drying beds where beautiful tobacco, grown from seedlings imported from Virginia, is developing an industry of great promise. Here there was one problem impossible to handle. A herd of something like a hundred great elephants had formed the habit of coming out on raiding expeditions from the hill forests and jungle, to the terrible destruction of the peasants' crops.

The terminus of our run was a considerable town that has grown up during the last few years in relation to the great irrigation development that the Dewan has put through. As we drove through the little town his eye was distressed by lack of tidiness and uniformity in the protective walls between the houses and the road, by the zinc-roofed porch of a wealthy gentleman's fine house and by the unfinished pavement. He flatly told the notables of the town when they met us that it gave him pain to see these slack inefficient elements in what might be a model borough. The town has as strong Hindu as Muslim communities. The leaders of both communities went with us to the mosque which the state had helped to build. Grievous defects in the structure had begun to show themselves. The community had discussed the matter and could see its way to some part of the repairs, but not to adequate reconstruction. Here again in a dense mass of town leaders in the porch of the mosque, with eager eyes glued upon the Dewan's face, the swift to-and-fro of discussion went on. He listened as always with impassive, attentive features, had a quiet word with his young leading officers to make sure of his ground, and then made the decision not only to help in the reconstruction but to give personally sufficient to line the summit of the dome with gold to give the mosque a similar grandeur to the Hindu temple. A terrific explosion of enthusiasm ensued, which the Dewan used to reiterate his distress about the draggled frontage of some of the houses, and even told the rich man that his zinc-roofed porch was an eyesore. 'I shall hope', he said, 'that when I come back in a month's time you will make my heart glad by having all these things put right.'

At one place we were entertained to what in India is called a breakfast but at Oxford would be known by the name of 'brunch', being half-way between breakfast and lunch. As we finished, the Dewan smiled at me mischievously like a schoolboy, and loaded himself with plantains, apples, sweets, and other odds and ends from the table. 'Now I am going to be generous at other people's expense', he laughed, and as we got into the car and small children crowded round to see him off, he gave every child within reach something to eat. The car was just moving off when he said, 'Stop. There is a very poor child.' With that extraordinary sensitiveness and swiftness of eye he had noticed, as none of the rest of us had, a little girl in absolute rags. He got out and handed to her all that remained in his hand of food and sweets, and we sped on to the next village.

I can say nothing of the villages of Mysore that I did not see, but there is no question that in the scores that I saw both on that day and on other journeys through Mysore independently, the children were plumper and better fed and the villages in general in cleaner trim than in any other part of India that I saw.

I can well believe that Sir Mirza has numerous enemies and detractors who can load his career with criticism, and obviously a system of direct decision by one man has its limitations. I was told, however, that in general his officers throughout the state take their cue from him, and that corruption is sharply limited by the knowledge that any man from any part of the state can get direct access to the Dewan if he has a grievance. It was piquant to swing from this detailed executive work in villages to talking over the Dewan's conversations with men like Sir Austen Chamberlain in London, where he has many friends, or Herr Ribbentrop in Berlin, and to discover a curiously happy co-operation with Mr. Gandhi tinged with positive affection. As might be expected, that affection and *camaraderie* do not extend to Jawaharlal Nehru, whose unconcealed determination to democratize and indeed socialize the Indian states makes him a natural political enemy. The Dewan was in England as a representative of Indian States at the Round Table Conferences, and in 1936 accompanied the Maharaja on his first visit there.

Sir Mirza's prolonged tenure of his office is due, of course, primarily to the confidence that His Highness the Maharaja of Mysore has in him. Their knowledge of each other extends from the days when they were boys together at the same school. The Maharaja is a devout Hindu, whose spiritual reality and catholicity of outlook came out in his address of welcome to the world conference on the problems of youth that was convened from Geneva by the World's Alliance of Y.M.C.A.s which he entertained with great liberality and sensitive hospitality early in 1937. Another evidence of this catholicity is that this Hindu prince should have around him a Muslim Dewan, a Christian Indian palace secretary, and an English private secretary who previously held high official appointments in the Madras Presidency.

Mysore State leads India in harnessing water power to the provision of electricity, not only for the cities but for many hundreds of villages. From the reservoir created by the longest dam in the world across the Cauvery River, irrigation water is carried to areas more than twenty miles away, and has made possible the phenomenal growth of sugar-cane and the manufacture of sugar.

The head of the Mysore municipality is pushing forward all the time co-ordinate schemes for slum clearance and housing. I saw what struck me as at once the cheapest and most comfortable homes for depressed class workers that I have seen in India, although those of the Bangalore Silk and Woollen Mills at Bangalore in the same state run them very close.

That the smouldering fires of religious animosity lie near the surface, even in a state where the communal tension with which the British are charged is absent, was shown while we were there by a frenzied outbreak of Muslims in Mysore who attempted to burn down a great Roman Catholic Church which was in course of construction, leading to the death of seven persons.

Inevitably with the new federal constitution, as the representatives of the Indian States sit side by side with liberal and socialist democrats, a certain measure of democratization is bound to set in in all these autocracies. Few of those who merely read about India and even of those who visit it realize what it means that one-third of that vast territory is under the rule of the Indian princes. There are seventy-five large and some five hundred small states. Some are the size of England and some are so tiny that the feudal chief can see the whole of his domain from his hill palace. It is, as we have already seen, one of the bitter criticisms of the British Government, made by liberals as well as by extremer nationalists, that we protect and support these outworn feudal despotisms which, apart from the British, would be inevitably either broken up or democratized. At their best, however, as we have seen in Mysore, there is something in this form of government that finds response in the Indian's passion for direct personal decision by his ruler, and his hatred of impersonal bureaucracy. It will be of great interest to watch how the spread of popular education affects the old *penchant* for autocracy.

In the person of Sir Akbar Hydari, the Finance Minister of His Highness the Nizam of Hyderabad, I met an interesting parallel to Sir Mirza Ismail. A devout Muslim of exquisite courtesy and a culture at once profound and delicate, Sir Akbar is the leading statesman in the greatest Indian state.

One unique experiment in Hyderabad State is the Osmania University. This rapidly growing university is the first attempt in India to give university education through a vernacular, English being a compulsory second language. I may say that it astonished me to discover in every part of India scholarly men who, if they have to make a speech in their own language, whether Urdu, Hindu, Telugu, Tamil, or what not, are obliged first to write it in English and then translate it, a psychological difficulty which throws a flood of light on the relative poverty of Indian cultural development in the last century. The one appalling difficulty which faces the Osmania University in this great adventure to turn the current against the results of Macaulay's Minute is obvious. To teach in Urdu history, philosophy, law, medicine, economics, pedagogics, zoology, &c., involves having the best text-books of the world on these subjects available in that language. The sheer work of translation itself would be titanic. The difficulty is made immensely greater, however, by the fact that in all those subjects an enormous number of the technical terms simply have no equivalent in Urdu, or indeed in any other Indian language. It is necessary therefore either to adopt those words or to create their Urdu equivalent. A large highly equipped staff embodied in what is called the Bureau of Translation is incessantly at work on this task. As I walked over the beautiful windswept plateau where the university is still in process of building, and watched the crowded classes and talked with some of their professors, I felt that here was one of the most important and significant cultural experiments in contemporary India. The most impressive evidence in favour of teaching in a vernacular is that students get a more thorough grasp, not simply of formulae learned by rote, but of the very substance of the subject. It is interesting to set on the other side the view, already recorded, of Professor Wadia in Mysore, that education in the vernacular is retrogressive because it leads to provincial rather than to national Indian loyalties, and therefore to a narrower outlook. It is to be remembered, however, that Urdu is known all over northern and mid-India.

Hyderabad is also forging ahead in the development of vocational education for specific technical occupations. The scheme is, after six years in primary schools and three in the lower secondary stage, for students to begin specialization in the industries and in agriculture, along with the pure arts.

In Hyderabad I felt at once the flavour of the old Mogul empire. Indeed the Nizam is a direct descendant of the Viceroy of the great Mogul emperor who conquered it. The tremendous fortress on the steep rocky hill near Hyderabad, the old cannon, the massive fort, all speak of the India of Queen Elizabeth's day. Although the ruler and one and a half million of his subjects are Muslims, eleven and a half million of the people are Hindu. Muslims have ruled Hyderabad for six hundred years. How self-sufficient the state is, is suggested by the fact that the Nizam has his own army, railway-system, and coinage. Indeed, his state is as large as Italy, while Hyderabad itself ranks as the third Muslim city of the world for size, coming only after Constantinople and Cairo.

Although in the city the minaret and the palace, with the Muslim architecture of other buildings, bring Islam all the time predominantly to the mind, within a few miles of the capital you are out in Hindu villages whose life remains extraordinarily unchanged. The ferment of nationalism makes practically no stir among them; the village is the centre of their life, and the little local temple of their worship, while their political loyalty hardly thinks of India at all; they are citizens of Hyderabad.

Yet ferments are at work, especially among the Muslim city population, most of all among women. The Director of Public Education told me that in his view purdah will be practically dead within another decade. The headmistress of a Girls' High School in

Hyderabad let me have an essay written by a seventeen-year-old Muslim girl. It is reproduced here as an impressive picture of the thoughtful, convinced way in which the new generation is working its path toward freedom, and it displays an ordered coherence of thought that many a western girl of that age might envy. After a description of purdah itself she goes on to say:

'It was thought to be of great value in making women ideal and faithful wives, so contributing to domestic happiness; but confinement indoors or going out closely veiled tells upon the health of women and makes them weak and unhealthy. It prevents the development of their individuality and the display of their talents, thereby making them entirely dependent upon men. It is a great drawback to their education. Nowadays there are purdah schools and clubs where ladies may learn to be sociable. But on account of men and women not mixing, women are shy and think it vulgar to meet and converse with men.

'The breakdown of purdah contributes to the building up of a nation. This statement can be proved from the recent history of Turkey and Iran. Some years ago Turkey was anxious lest she should be outstripped by Greece. The part played by women contributed to Turkey's recovery. Khalida Adeeb Kanum, one of Turkey's leading women, told us in her lecture why Turkey had broken purdah. She pointed out that God has created both man and woman, and if these two cannot get to know one another by meeting freely, their nation cannot progress. Lately Iran has followed the example of Turkey since they see that the results of breaking purdah have been so beneficial.

'God has given woman every power and talent, so why should she not take part in public affairs when she has intelligence to do so. Women are generally wise, and can help men in the affairs of the home, the state, and the world.

It is essential that we should break purdah if we wish to become a leading nation.'

The great need of the Indian States, as indeed of India as a whole, is obviously for leadership and a civil service of real integrity and efficiency. In this connexion I recall that an educationist who has lived in Hyderabad for a good many years was told on his arrival that there were three leading officers in that state on whose word he could absolutely rely and know that it would be carried out, and that they were above all corruption. The educationist found that this was so, and it was only after he had got to know them personally over some years that he discovered that all three of them (and they include Sir Akbar Hyderi himself) spent the formative years of their boyhood in the atmosphere and surrounded by the standard of values of a Christian school.

It is clear that the future of these hundreds of states covering an area one-third of the size of Europe is intimately bound up with the destiny of the Indian peoples as a whole. The attitude of the princes to the new constitution is obviously made complex by the fact, on the one hand, of their reluctance to come so far into the federal system as to lose the almost sovereign autocracy they now exercise, and on the other hand, by their fear that, if the new constitution breaks down, they may have their power swept away in obedience to a policy such as that outlined by Jawaharlal Nehru in his presidential address to the National Congress in December 1936. The Indian States, he said, will have to fit into a scheme of a free India, and their peoples must have the same personal, civil, and democratic liberties as those of the rest of India.

CHAPTER XII

The Beauty of Ajanta

THE most modern creation that I saw in India was the most ancient. The immortal loveliness of the teeming life of men and women, animals and flowers of the frescoes in the caves of Ajanta, although painted at intervals between the third century before Christ and the sixth century of the Christian era, are of the very essence of to-day and to-morrow just because they are timeless. 'The ageless fecundity, the endless going on of life' overwhelmed me in those caves even more than in the teeming cities and villages themselves, and while sharing the perpetual pilgrimage of the Indian roads. For here in these caves art such as has no parallel in Asia (and has only been equalled here and there in Europe—as in the Sistine Chapel) has caught in a single net the kinship of the life of man with that of the wild animals and plants; and has expressed the subtle penetration of all earth's creatures and flowers and fruits with the Spirit from whose creative energy they spring. Nothing else in the art of Asia rises to the supreme heights of creation achieved by those anonymous Buddhist monk-artists in the temples hewn in the volcanic rock of their remote cliff-valley of Ajanta.

The gracious hospitality of the State of Hyderabad, expressed through the sensitive courtesy of Sir Akbar Hydari, made our visit to Ajanta possible, and transformed what would have been an arduous enterprise into a joyful adventure into a new world of creative art. For Ajanta is just on forty miles from the nearest railway station and has no town of any size near to it. To be a guest of the government more than wiped out all difficulties. A car was at Jalgaon station on the arrival of the train from Bombay at dawn. We were driven to the Nizam's guest house near the caves, where the service, the food, and the accommodation expressed the thoughtful consideration of oriental hospitality at its best. Khan Bahadur Syed Ahmed, the artist-archaeologist who has given years to the preservation and the reproduction of the pictures, took us to the caves and with his assistant spent the day and the following morning in careful and enthusiastic interpretation of the sculpture and the paintings. Nor did the care of our hosts cease until we were again at Jalgaon *en route* for Allahabad. It is not easy adequately to express gratitude for one of the outstanding experiences of a lifetime.

After travelling over the rolling landscape of this north-west corner of the Nizam's dominions, there was a certain delightful shock of astonishment in coming upon a beautiful deep valley carved out of the hills by a rapidly running stream. We climbed steps hewn on one side of the valley and suddenly came upon what W. E. Gladstone Solomon describes as 'that tremendous scimitar of columned temples, athwart the face of the precipice, four furlongs from the boss of the hilt to the point of the blade'. Far down at the foot of the cliff the stream fills the valley with the living voice of running water. As I walked along in front of the entrancing entrances to the twenty-nine temples, my eyes were drawn even from their beauty by the curve of the river valley that here moves sharply southward till arrested by the white spray of a waterfall cascading over a precipice. The harsh volcanic cliff-crags are festooned with shrub and creeper and wild flowers. Here more than twenty-two centuries ago Buddhist monks came to meditate upon the Way in a lovely place, remote from the ambition and the fears of the world of affairs, yet not cut off either from nature or from the life of peasant India. Indeed the pageant seemed to come to life as I stood on the long balcony hewn in the rock where lizards basked in the blazing sunshine, and watched Indian women in artless procession, the brilliant blues and reds, the delicate creams and pinks of their saris in lovely relief against the rock of the temple façades.

Here the monks worked out in stone one of the greatest creations of the mind. The marvel of the carved façades of the rock-hewn cave-temples would make one stand outside absorbed in their proportions and detail were it not for the surpassing loveliness of what lies hidden within. The front of the first cave has its sculptured men, its architraves of spirited elephants, its hunting scenes and lively human figures, which are a fitting introduction to the frescoes within. For sheer joy of living, by some miracle of sustained creativity, runs through all the pictures, painted as they were through century after century by master after master. The Sistine Chapel expresses the personal genius of a supreme artist; at Ajanta I felt that the spirit of a race had conspired to capture and express not only the human drama, but the eternal creative design into which the Great Artificer has wrought the world of nature and the triumph of the spirit.

Most of the pictures tell the Jatala stories. These are the legends of the earthly life of the Buddha in his many existences on earth incarnate (as Bodhisattva) either in man or animal, as pigeon, as a golden goose, or king of the monkeys. This alone makes these pictures unique in Buddhist art. In China and Japan the art of Buddhist masters is concentrated upon the meditative life of the Buddha. At Ajanta the young virile artists throbbed with absorption in the pulsating life of this world.

I stand before the Lotus-handed Bodhisattva. The stalwart trunk with the flush of young blood under the brown skin, the muscular neck set on wide shoulders carrying a manly head, with full lips compressed in quiet decision under the long, straight nose; his thoughtful, contemplative eyes looking down under arched brows, and the lofty forehead crowned with the jewelled head-dress of the prince—all show the spiritual happily regnant in the physical. There is perfection in the blend of grace and strength in the firm unfaltering curves of shoulder and elbow and wrist. The long black hair flowing down behind the shoulders and the simple sparse dress from the loins downward reveal the young prince as having shaken off luxury in the practice of simplicity. The right hand, every curve of whose every finger is masterly, holds up the blue lotus that marks the pure in heart.

At his left sits his dark consort, her almost black face lovely in its natural simplicity; the curves of the body instinct with the poise and dignity of unconscious modesty, the modelling of cheek and nose and mouth and the thoughtful eyes and shapely ears all suggested by some miracle of light and shade that marks the swift flawless brushwork of a master-hand. Her hand too holds a lotus. The pearls on her head shed a soft radiance so real as to be almost incredible in painting that has survived at least fourteen centuries. As is the case with the women and girls in so many of these pictures, you have a nudity that is unlike that of the consciously posed bodies of European art. It is completely natural and unnoticed; the normal everyday way of life in the warm air of India. Indeed, of all the women's figures in the pictures it may be truly said that you can never trace in them any pose. They convey no sense of consciousness of being painted; the artists seem to catch this gesture, that natural way of standing or sitting without the subject's knowledge. It may well be that no women or girls ever posed for them, that the monk caught in the mesh of his memory some fleeting gesture and immortalized it.

On the Bodhisattva's right is his wand-bearer, dark, sturdy, proud of his office yet subordinate to his prince, wearing the light-coloured robe of his rank. We tear our eyes from the central group and go in detail over the crowded background and foreground of the picture. There is a radiant joy in the creation that recalls the exclamation of God in the first chapter of Genesis as He looked on the animals and plants and man—'Behold it was very good'. On the hills in the background are monkeys leaping for joy fearless of the splendid lions. A gorgeous peacock with open beak cries his love aloud to the listening pea-hen. A musician plays a *vina*. Two lovers half concealed among the trees look out on the Prince. Behind the wand-bearer a queenly figure 'black but comely' lounges in happy abandon. The whole scene is crowded with life. One might expect an atmosphere of chaotic disorder in such unstudied grouping. On the contrary, by some strange alchemy a lovely natural unity is called into harmonious being. I know no picture of any age or land that so perfectly reveals man, virile, spiritual, intellectual, resting naturally in the heart of the creation of which he is the crown. For the Prince looks out on it all, having made his own inner discipline of will, not with an attitude of superiority and command, with no aloofness. Although separated by the soul within him from the animal life that throngs around, his loving-kindness takes the world into his compassion.

When I withdrew my mind from wonder at this unique expression in art of the coherence of all life and from joy in its radiant lithe profusion, the spirit of wonder again played about the colours. It is known that many of the colours were ground from the rock upon and within the cliffs. Indeed I picked up a number of shining pieces of green mineral from the cliff-edge. But, so far as I know, the secret of the mixing of those colours to secure their miraculous permanence has so far eluded both the artist and the chemist of today; although while I was there fractional pieces of the colour were being confided to expert chemists to try by analysis to recover their composition. The reds alone baffle yet amaze: they burn, they gently smoulder; they glow like blood under the skin; they are radiant like wine; they sink to the quiet of rusty lichen on a fallen tree. I let my eyes rest on the blues of the peacock; and found them straying to the deep green of the shrubs that almost hide yet only serve more subtly to reveal him and his attentive mate. And with what consummate art the almost black brownness of the consort and of the amorous woman behind the official throws into relief the bloom of youth on the prince's lighter skin.

The varied comedy and tragedy of the human drama came into the orbit of these strange monks who may have been withdrawn from the world, but whose hearts certainly shared the suffering and happiness of men. Sympathy, love-making, fighting, courage, humour, coyness, heartbreak are all expressed but never emphasized. I was deeply moved by this all-embracing compassion as I moved from temple to temple and from picture to picture. To watch the dying princess, drooping in the loving solicitous arms of her attendant maid, with the expressions of grief, wonder, hope; and then turn to the Raja sporting affectionately with his consort in a palace scene where the attendant girls have the grace and lively beauty of Botticelli's 'Primavera'; and from that go on to watch the expectancy in the upturned faces of mother and daughter as they supplicate before the Buddha is to realize how rich was the interpretative understanding of those early anonymous artists.

Most intense of all in its dramatic strength is the picture-sequence of the Temptation of the Buddha. The Bodhisattva is seated under the sacred tree and is nearing the hour of supreme Enlightenment through which he will pass to Buddhahood. The Spirit of Evil, Mara, whose work will be foiled if the path of salvation should thus be opened to men, mobilizes the lust for power and the longing for pleasure. Mara's daughters in wanton abandon throw themselves before the Bodhisattva to wile him away to the pleasures of the flesh. He resists their allurements. Mara, infuriated, calls up his demon-forces who hurl themselves toward their victim to throw him from his seat. The Bodhisattva, in virtue of merit acquired in previous existences—whose story is told in the other pictures—calls on the Earth-goddess to exercise her power, whereat she puts the demons to flight. It was in the night following the temptation that enlightenment came, the hour of the birth of Buddhism into the world.

As I stand before the exquisite power and grace of the picture that has at its heart a black princess, another source of wonder breaks on me. She sits there, her head, with its black hair, firm nose, and full lips, that would have been sensual had they not been dominated by a disciplined spirit, bent down quietly thinking out some enigma. She is essential woman. As Captain Gladstone Solomon of the Bombay School of Art writes: 'I can think of no parallel to this frank and chivalrous woman-worship of Ajanta. Nowhere else perhaps has woman received such perfect and understanding homage.' Gay, charming, carefree woman in those pictures never fails of her dignity and grace. Even that marvellous girl-princess standing carelessly leaning against a wall, one leg bent sharply up at the knee so that the sole of her foot is against the wall, in an attitude in which I saw many Indians during the three months in the land, is exquisite in her insouciance. Ropes and pendants of pearls form her sole raiment. Nothing in all these pictures is more unexpected or delightful than the adornments of the women and girls —beaten work in gold and silver, coronals of flowers catching up a chignon; looped knots of hair into which flowers are woven; peacock feather tips, and everywhere and always the liquid radiance of pearls.

Broken and dimmed as many of the pictures are, and demanding long, quiet meditation before they deliver all their meaning or compel one with the steady fragrance of their beauty, these hundreds of pictures, rising from the ground to some twenty or thirty feet high and spread in wide vistas to the left and right along the rock-hewn walls of the cave-temples, offer a sustained triumph of creative art such as I have never seen before and never expect to see surpassed.

The imagination staggers under the effort either to grasp or to begin to express the triumphant balance of the whole achievement. I look all along the lovely crescent-moon curve of the sculptured façades as they stretch away along the cliff front looking out over the river valley. I remember with wonder how from the seventh century until some British soldiers passed that way in the nineteenth century they were wholly hidden from the world by jungle-growth. The sculptures speak the dignity and grace of man and woman, the multiform richness and vitality of beast and bird. About it all floats the atmosphere of a benign spiritual presence that loves created nature while brooding over it, apart but not aloof. Then I enter one of the twenty-nine temples and see away at the other end of the dimness, floodlit by a hidden lamp held by an attendant Indian, the quiet meditative majesty of a gigantic figure of the seated Buddha, with the fingers of one hand touched by a finger of the other, in the attitude of the teacher. He has been seated there for at least fifteen centuries. Around the walls are some of the pictures that I have tried to describe.

I move from temple to temple; from beauty to beauty, whether of frescoe or sculpture; for hour after hour. And although the decay of two millennia has worked its corrosion on some of them, and none is in its pristine perfection, the power of that harmonious conception grows on the spirit. Here is drama of human life in palace and garden, city and courtyard and on the battlefield, played in the living presence of the spirit, against the riotous background of the jungle, the forest, and the plain. The grace of the deer, the strength of the elephant, the loveliness of bird and flower, with the loves and hates of man, his griefs and joys, weave the stuff of this earth's life across the woof of spiritual reality.

CHAPTER XIII

Whither?

As I stood on the veranda at Erode and saluted Mr. E. V. Ramaswami Naikkar, his leonine head with its rebellious mass of curly iron-grey hair and bushy beard, the strong nose, full lips, and the challenging gleam in the eyes carried me back to the day when my father took me as a school-boy to hear William Morris lecture on socialism. The resemblance, I was to discover in the next two or three hours, went much deeper than external likeness. For this Indian William Morris of the twentieth century has the same readiness to tilt a lance at any stale convention, the same prodigal pouring out of eager challenge to evil custom and of effort for a brave new world. In place of the powder-blue shirt and navy suit with the strong steel watch-chain that I recall William Morris wearing, the Indian warrior of ideas was wearing the simple cotton tunic and dhoti of contemporary India. The title of his foolscap-size periodical *Revolt*, a bound volume of which for a whole year I have with me, makes a good title actually for his life-story. A wild rebellious youth, member of a well-to-do land-owning family, he caught the flame from that revolutionary who has spiritualized so many rebels, Mr. Gandhi. He became a disciple of his, gave up his wild practices, and joined Congress. Meanwhile, so vigorous was his local leadership that he became the chairman of the Erode municipality. He was elected president of the Congress committee for the whole Tamil area of India. In jail for a year in the 1921 non-co-operation movement, he came out a rebel against the Brahmin domination of the Congress movement. So he flung himself into a left-wing fight, as leader in the Justice party. This, however, was too mild for him. He created a 'ginger group' of young people called the Self-Respect movement. His intense loathing of Brahmin domination in social and political life led him from stage to stage in attacks first on the Roman Catholic confessional and then on all religion. Travelling to Europe he was hailed with immense enthusiasm in Moscow and came back to India an enthusiastic believer in the Russian experiment and fiery in his anti-religious fanaticism. His flaming attacks on Islam and Christianity and the seditious strength of his communist enthusiasm led to the temporary suppression of his periodical and his own imprisonment. Finding his uncompromising vehemence too strong even for his readers, his attitude has modified, and he stands to-day as the head and front of the effort in the south to free Congress from the stranglehold of its conservative elements. When I visited him next day in his office and printing works combined I found his photograph on the wall between the photographs of Lenin and Bernard Shaw. The products of his press do not equal those of the Kelmscott Press, but the use of a privately owned press for the propagation of his ideas added another to the curious parallelisms between Mr. Ramaswami Naikkar and William Morris.

There joined us on the veranda the headmaster of a Hindu high school who is a devotee of Nehru and a practitioner of *yoga*; and alongside him the local cinema film magnate who is a follower of Gandhi. The men were all eager, able, well-read Hindus, thoroughly competent to defend the positions they held; and, as we have seen, each sharply differing in many respects from the others—agreeing only in their desire for the end of British rule in India.

By standing aside from the actual discussion, yet initiating and giving occasional guidance to it with questions on the trends of the day in India, I was able to listen-in for hours to men who were not telling the stranger what they wished him to believe but threshing out with each other their real convictions.

When at last we parted late in the evening with the three trends that they represented firmly in my mind, the headmaster, at my desire, stayed for a while to let me experience one or two examples of *yoga* exercises. Placing a rug on the floor he proceeded to stand on his head. Now to any Englishman the idea of a headmaster standing on his head is thoroughly comic. Yet on the contrary, as he wound his dhoti round his legs and then, with his head and elbows on the ground slowly and without any jerk, by sheer muscular control and poise raised his body and his legs until he stood perfectly still on his head, the whole act had a curiously moving and almost devotional significance. The beauty of control, balance, even meditative calm pervaded it. He told me that he would often stand for twenty minutes like that early in the morning, with great benefit to spirit and mental efficiency as well as to bodily health. So the act was an element in achieving equilibrium of personality. He then sat on the rug, crossed his legs on his stomach, with the soles of the feet upwards, in the attitude of the Buddha, and heaving forward over his crossed legs touched the ground with his forehead. The only humour that I found in this lay in imagining some headmasters whom I know in the West trying to achieve even the first movement in this exercise. The second amusement lay in discovering by trial that, simple as the manœuvre looked when he executed it, it demanded a whole series of disciplines, with flexibility and muscular control.

I can think of no experiences to, which my mind returns with greater zest than the experiences of unnumbered discussions in such groups in every part of India. They varied in numbers from three to thirty. For instance, I recall a senior group with the Director of Public Education of one of the Indian States, its ex-Chief Justice, its Attorney-General, all Muslims, a zealous theosophist, and a man, a Hindu by birth, hotly opposed to all forms of institutional religion. They expounded not simply their own attitudes, though these emerged, but the perspective of change that they saw coming over the new generation. The greater majority of the groups, however, were composed of that new generation, some of them students even in their first year, while some looked at things from the longer perspective of a post-graduate course. I remember one such group of about ten men of this standing who were studying respectively economics, literature, philosophy, psychology, and theology. Religiously they were Hindu, Parsi, and Christian. In background they came from villages and cities and from very different grades of society. One of the Christians, at any rate, had come up from the depressed classes. In other groups men and women students discussed together, for instance, questions relating to the control of parents over children in the old family system, the tension arising from the desire of youth for self-determination, and, most novel in

India, the problem presented by the desire to choose one's own husband or wife in an environment where so little chance of social contact between the sexes exists. In other groups were young village school teachers, university professors, lawyers, politicians, and young men in business.

Among the other subjects—most of them loaded with dynamite in such a land as India to-day—which I got these groups to discuss, were the trends in political life, such as the problem whether social and economic revolution must or must not go with the political rebellion against imperialism; or again, whether men shall turn their backs on Hinduism as on all organized religion and seize modern scientific techniques with both hands, or, as with the followers of Gandhi, hurl themselves into a crusade to reform Hinduism from within and protect the soul of India against the corrosions of western materialism. No problem again is more charged with passion in India than that of one's attitude to people of other faiths. The missionary enterprise of Hinduism to call back into the fold Muslims or Christians who have left their ancestral faith, the painful tensions created when multitudes of the depressed classes threaten to turn their backs on the temple at the very hour when Gandhi's Harijan movement, as we have seen, is in a life and death struggle to open its gates to the outcaste—all this is exacerbated by the fact that the new constitution makes religious conversion the equivalent of the transfer of political votes.

These questions were, so to speak, the electric starters which set the discussions going. In those discussions personal experiences of, for instance, the joint family system, were thrown into the pool to enforce arguments on the one side or the other. All unconsciously, through the sheer zest of the groups' examination of their own lives and the changes going on in youth around them, the new India revealed itself. How complex and many-sided the trends toward that new India are, the analysis we are now going to attempt can only broadly suggest. There can surely never have been any hour in India's long history when so many ferments have been thrust into the stuff of her life. To catch glimpses of those leavens at their transforming work among these marvellous peoples is one of the most fascinating adventures that has ever been open to the mind of man.

One conclusion arising out of this experience I have tested, without contradiction, on every kind of man from the left wing of Congress to the stiffest bureaucrat. It is that the mind of India is swinging from the contemplation of revolution on purely political lines to the goal of economic revolution on socialist, if not even Marxian, principles. This, of course, is part of the world movement that has carried, for instance, the Rooseveltian government in U.S. into economic planning for the whole country, and makes the development and control of its economic life both internally and in world relations a major preoccupation of every government in Europe. It is a far more revolutionary stage in an ancient static economic civilization like that of India. In the mind of men like Jawaharlal Nehru, the wealthy absentee landlord, the money-lender with his economic stranglehold on the peasant, and the despotic Indian prince are obstacles to the new free socialist republic of India whose elimination is as necessary as is the removal of the power of the British government. In terms of personality this trend is dramatically illustrated by the swing of popular favour that has set Jawaharlal Nehru in the centre of the stage of India's revolutionary movement, relegating Gandhi at least for the time being to a secondary role.

Western education and ways of life are battering on the walls of the immemorial joint family system and breaking down the seclusion of woman, whether Muslim or Hindu. The Princess Durru Shehvar, married to the heir of the throne of the greatest Muslim state in India, stood, with no veil over her face, a week or so before I got to Hyderabad, delivering a presidential address to the Hyderabad State Women's Conference,[1] stirring them to 'Let your ambition strive to remove the legal and social disabilities that stand in your way: let your ability prove the supreme justification of that removal', and proclaiming the gospel to India of 'the economic independence of its women'. She is the beautiful daughter of the exiled Sultan of Turkey, the deposed Caliph of all Islam. 'Women', she went on, 'must be taught the dignity of work. Every woman ought to be in a position to support herself by means of an honourable livelihood should the occasion arise. . . . To-day women in almost every civilized country of the world are no longer parasites of dependence but citizens of the soil that has bred them—with the right to exist, to take, and to give; with the right to add to the honour of their nation and the ethics of their people; with the courage and knowledge to exalt and develop the common cause of progress.'

Ten years ago that event would have been impossible in India: and it would have been equally fantastic to imagine such a leader pressing publicly, as the Princess did, for free compulsory universal primary education in

[1] October 30th, 1936.

Hyderabad, which has been backward in its literacy in comparison with most of India.

When one meets, in the drawing-rooms of Lahore, Muslim husbands and wives enjoying Christmas festivities and sees them flocking to the cinemas, or when one sees in the select restaurants of the cities of India that 50 per cent of the folk enjoying afternoon tea are women where barely two per cent would have gone out ten years ago, you witness just two or three of the thousands of indications of what is perhaps the most momentous of all the changes taking place in India's life.

Against this trend of advance the forces of conservatism are exercising all their power. There is a strong undertow beneath the advancing tide. I even heard of Muslim men buying pictures of bathing scenes on the beaches of Europe in order to shock their womenfolk back into seclusion away from the, to them, outrageous immodesty thus portrayed. It comes with somewhat of a shock to discover highly educated men strongly preferring their wives to stay in purdah. A professor in English in Osmania University asked two hundred of his students to write on the theme, 'Should girls be educated?' He told his students to say just what they felt; the papers would be marked, not on the views expressed, but on the quality of the English language used to convey them. The odd and unexpected result was that the views were divided, half and half, into the two extremes. One side wanted women out without any restrictions in co-educational universities and colleges, with all the barriers down; others held that women's sole duty was domestic. One romantic boy said that woman's place was 'to comfort her husband when he comes back from battle'. A highly educated Brahmin Hindu, who reads widely in western literature, vigorously advocated child marriage and the seclusion of women in a talk with me. He gave as his reasons that every girl from eleven years upwards inevitably develops 'mischievous tendencies'. Seeing also that, in his own words, 'all men are bad', there was no alternative to early marriage and seclusion.

I brought this matter up with at least a score of groups of students in north, south, east, and west of India. The students were Hindu, Muslim, and Christian. Everywhere they asserted that a tension, often painful, exists between the old authority of the family, especially as vested in the parents and the uncles, and their own desire for freedom. In one college where I was staying a youth, on the eve of his examination, received a postcard from his father telling him his marriage had been arranged and calling him home immediately. A night spent by the youth in bitter weeping was followed by his going home immediately, his student career shattered. On the other hand, a sexagenarian Hindu lamented to me that, as he put it, 'to-day the father of the family is just the family donkey on whom the boys and girls of the family go for a joy ride'. Unquestionably the cream of India's womanhood desire to share freedom and access to the beauty and drama of the world, while sustaining that poise and unconscious dignity that come from loyalty to values of goodness, truth, and beauty.

So much of personal economic security and moral control has been vested for centuries in the joint family system that its passing unquestionably, in proportion as it occurs, creates new tensions. The old Hindu family system stands for authoritative relationships of father and son, and the choice by the elders of husband and wife; it provides insurance against unemployment and sickness; it gives guidance in the sequence of life decisions that come to every man. As the old system gives way to freedom and individualism all these powerful aids to social solidarity will need reinforcement from other quarters. The old system with its powerful sense of social responsibility sacrificed the individual's self-expression for the good of the group; the vehement new individualism from the West may, if untempered, lead to anarchic selfishness.

In the region of religion two apparently contradictory trends really have at least one source in common. On the one side is the burning intensification of loyalties to the religious communities to which men belong, quickened by the communal award which gives political value to the number of heads to be counted as Muslim, Hindu, Sikh, or Christian. On the other side is a sharp, rather harsh rise of antagonism to all organized religion, although not necessarily to a spiritual view of reality. Almost universally among Indians the blame for this intensity of communal antagonism is laid on the shoulders of the British government. The prevailing view is that the British of malice aforethought applied the principle 'divide and rule' to the existing antagonisms of Hindu and Muslim. Large numbers go even further and deny that these antagonisms were active previous to the British fomenting of them. Specially intense criticism is directed against Mr. Ramsay MacDonald for having made the Communal Award. It seems quite useless to state and restate the argument, first, that these antagonisms actually date back to earlier centuries and, second, that no authoritative scheme for any other plan of representation has ever been put forward by India in terms that have not been repudiated by one or other powerful group.

The repercussion on religion itself is harmful, for it tends to give membership of one or other of the religious communities a political significance. A man or a woman tends to be counted as a vote rather than as a sincere follower. For this reason I was more than once eagerly approached by young students or graduates with the statement that their repudiation of the traditional faiths was caused by their ardent desire for spiritual truth. I scanned about eighty essays written by Hindu, Muslim, and Christian students in Travancore on religion in the new India. The essays were anonymous so that there was no attempt to impress the professor with the student's loyalty to any particular view. Practically all were perplexed and bewildered, with a small notable group from each of the faiths who had found clear guidance for life. A few repudiated even a spiritual view of the universe, but a clear majority took the position just stated, that it was essential to get past the loyalty to traditional formulae to some spiritual reality. This really accounts for the considerable popularity of theosophist teaching. 'If I leave Hinduism', a young Indian graduate of Oxford put it earnestly to me, 'in search of reality, I am more loyal to spiritual values than is the Hindu boy who is led by his parents from one ceremony of initiation to another, blind to their meaning, and only led by brainless obedience to the custom of his caste. The fact that young folk often owe no loyalty to organized religion is really due to their wish to get to the heart of spiritual reality.'

One almost disastrous weakness of nine-tenths of the discussion of movements in India to-day is the result of the intense preoccupation of Indians with their own problems. You would imagine that India and Britain were alone as in a kind of vacuum flask. I was even told that it was unfair to suggest such considerations when I remarked that Japan's reiterated public claim to be 'the guardian of Asia' included intense interest in India, and that the withdrawal of the British navy would leave India 'the richest booty on earth' and a prey to hungry imperialisms either of the east or of the west. Yet, realistically considered, they appear to me to be of the very essence of the problem of India's free and united future. Similarly, the movements in prices of raw materials which are bleeding millions of India's peasantry white are obviously largely the product of world economic trends, but are laid at the door of men sitting behind desks in Delhi and Whitehall.

I was startled in this connexion by an unexpected by-product of a few paragraphs in a talk that I gave to a considerable group of students. I mentioned in a description of youth movements round the world the steps taken by the Japanese government to arrest large numbers of students, not for having done anything wrong but for having 'Dangerous Thoughts'. What astonished and interested them was the fact that students in Japan, Italy, and Germany, not to speak of Russia, would be arrested for critical attacks on their own governments no more scathing than those freely made with impunity by students in India of the British rule which they would describe as 'tyrannical'. One of the greatest needs of Indian life is to open all her windows so that she may get a realistic picture of the titanic forces playing around her in the world, both of the West and of the Far East. In this connexion part of Jawaharlal Nehru's presidential address to Congress while I was in India struck a new note of more than passing interest. He pleaded for international thinking for India, and the planning of an international policy:

'We are all engrossed in India at present in the provincial elections that will take place soon. The congress has put up over a thousand candidates and this business of election ties us up in many ways, and yet I would ask you . . . to take heed of the terrible and fascinating drama of the world. Our destinies are linked up with it, and our fate, like the fate of every country, will depend on the outcome of the conflicts of rival forces and ideas that are taking place everywhere. Again I would remind you that our problem of national freedom as well as social freedom is but a part of this great world problem, and to understand ourselves we must understand others also.'

I remember years ago in Palestine asking a leading British official why our government did not grapple with a certain problem. 'Our policy', he said, 'is always to let sleeping dogs lie.' I could not help suggesting that that was not the true metaphor, but that what we were doing was to let tiger cubs grow, which has unfortunately proved to be the truth. The most dramatic thing about the British government in India to-day is the fight within it between the tendency that lets sleeping dogs lie and the newer line of taking the initiative to grapple with a problem in its early stages. Lord Linlithgow's concern for rural reconstruction is one of these hopeful initiatives. When, as in Sir John Anderson's action in setting Mr. Mitter to economic planning for Bengal, it harnesses first-class Indian ability to the task, the benefit is doubled. The rapid Indianization of the services is another aspect of this same movement. It is unfortunate that enthusiastic nationalists often deride men who go into the services as mere lap-dogs and seekers after the loaves and fishes, in a sense traitors to their country's cause. Low motives may actuate many, but India will be in a tragic mess if, as Home Rule comes, she has no civil service equipped to run the machine. In this connexion the best piece of statesmanlike thinking that I have seen from an Indian nationalist during the time in India was shown in the articles by Mr. Subash Chandra Bose in the *Hindustan Times*, arguing strongly that Congress should set to work to discover and train talent in international affairs. For if it ever hopes to run the country in a world full of international and inter-racial pitfalls a trained diplomatic service is a prime essential. Mr. Bose's relatively innocent book, *The Indian Struggle*, is still proscribed and refused entry into India. He himself is interned and refused all visitors from outside; he was the one person in India whom the government declined to let me visit.

One rather tragic effect of growing Indianization is still further to penalize the large Anglo-Indian community. Accepted neither by the Indian nor by the British, they have been driven socially and even economically in on themselves. Certain occupations, notably that of railway officials, for which they were educationally and by language capacity well fitted, were in the past largely reserved for them. The process of Indianization of the services, however, is pushing them out. An intensely difficult dilemma is thus set before them. These economic positions can only be theirs by identification with the Indian community, and their whole trend, on the contrary, has been toward the European side of life, culturally and socially. One curious social tension arises from the fact that the Anglo-Indian girls are extremely attractive to young European men, and often the ambition of the girls is to marry a European and thus enter the community. The European, however, rarely intends marriage. The situation ends in the infuriation of the Anglo-Indian young men and the tragic disillusionment of the girls.

The government horizon in India is, of course, filled with problems of the working of the new constitution. Just as the dilemma—to co-operate or not to co-operate—dominates the mind of Congress, so the question—will the constitution be worked or wrecked?—fills much of the thought of government, as has been indicated again and again in this book.

In my own mind, as I think I have already said, the most disquieting feature of British rule in India to-day is that to the enormous majority of peasants the one aspect of government they are conscious of is the activity of the tax-collector, and to all students the eavesdropping and spying by the payment of sneaks who report seditious talk. The vast ameliorative services of irrigation and health, afforestation and justice are obscured behind the face of the tax-collector and the police spy. This makes it all the more unfortunate that Nehru, as in his presidential speech to Congress, when talking of famine, flood, and drought should go out of his way to assert that the Government does not concern itself with these things, when the fact is, as he must surely know, that it has done more than any other rule on earth—more even than the United States in its own territory—to fight these things, and has in point of fact made famine impossible by an interrelation of transport and irrigation. *Suppressio veri* and still less *suggestio falsi* will not aid the cause of Indian freedom.

One very important trend in India's life, as we have already seen, is the new interest in the villager. Interest in him ranges from the British Government, headed by the Viceroy's policy of rural reconstruction, to Congress. Mr. Gandhi's preoccupation with the peasant-farmer is well known. There is a new stirring also within the life of the villagers themselves, even among the lowest castes and depressed classes. They have suddenly become of importance in the political scheme. Politicians angle for their votes, the agitator goes among them stirring up discontent. They may not know very much of what it is all about, but they are beginning to realize that *karma*, the inexorable working of fate, is not a sufficient explanation of the state of semi-starvation and joylessness in which millions of them are kept. They see a glimmer of hope of changing their hard lot. Travel by train and more particularly by motor-bus is beginning to widen their horizon. The younger men go to the cinema in the nearest town, and through them news of the larger world—probably in a very garbled form—filters through to the villages. This is not to say that there is at present any startling change in the immemorial life of the village, but there are signs of a stirring. Even the Singer sewing machine—and one may be found in most of the larger villages—and the kerosene oil tin, which in its time plays many parts from that of roofing to water-vessel, are signs of the gradual penetration of change. The leap from the tiny earthenware lamp with a wick of thread soaked in oil to electric light has been made in some places. In Mysore State, for instance, a great hydro-electric plant supplies electricity to villages at an infinitesimal charge, so that it is within the reach of all but the very poorest. Similar enterprises have been started in other parts where water-power is available.

The record of village improvement in Nasik district is illuminating. A report on this work, that is fostered by Lord Brabourne in Bombay Presidency, states:

'The villager would not like it if it meant only that persons alien to him in outlook and method of life descended on him and told him to be like themselves. But this is not what actually happens. The villager is backward not because he likes it but because he has no opportunity of being anything else. His chief failing is the inability to combine. The Village Improvement Movement helps him to combine and get things done and generally he likes it and its results.'

The report goes on to say that the most successful work is that which has been done by the villagers themselves. Among other things they combine to clean up the villages, build latrines, deepen wells, subscribe half the pay of a master for a new school, and build new school houses.

Broadcasting, again, though still in its infancy in India and heavily handicapped in many ways, may at any time, if facilities are given for its development, become a potent force for the education of the illiterate masses who could not be reached in any other way. Long talks in Delhi with Mr. Lionel Fielden, the enthusiastic and able Director of Broadcasting, convinced me of the enormous potentialities of this medium of communication and instruction, although I realized with sympathy the obstacles at present in the path of Mr. Fielden and his colleagues. Even so, broadcasting has its successes as a disseminator of new ideas. In response to talks to farmers, offering better seed as part of the Government's policy of reconstruction, numbers of letters were received from interested listeners. And in the community of Indian village life, one interested listener may mean dozens, for every scrap of news is passed on to other men, discussed from every angle, and pondered over.

The fact that in Delhi alone 2,500 of the registered listeners are small clerks leads Mr. Fielden to look forward to nothing short of five million listeners in a relatively short time. The subscriptions to the *Indian Listener* are now running from 16,000 upwards. The problem of re-charging batteries in remote villages is met by sending a lorry round. Mr. Fielden finds, curiously enough, that the village hour has a great appeal to the people of the towns. This is accounted for by the universal popularity of folk songs and the fact that he has developed a humorous equivalent of Mutt and Jeff or Amos and Andy.

The four short-wave stations now being developed will be heard in Lhasa, the capital of Tibet, Teheran, the capital of Iran, Sinkiang on the western edge of China, and in Afghanistan. For years I have been convinced that all across Asia broadcasting opens an entirely new era of education and of contact between government and people. For the first time in history it is possible for a ruler to get into direct touch with the people throughout the whole of his dominions, without travel and even though they cannot read. Two of the progressive Indian states, Mysore and Hyderabad, already are using this medium. I saw on great open lawns in Mysore city some thousands of people listening to a programme in which the ever-popular Indian music was interspersed with short talks on practical expressions of citizenship, including the care of children, the cleanliness of the city, and so on. In Hyderabad, again, broadcasting is being experimented with as a tool of adult education. The work of agitators who foment unrest among villagers who are ignorant and superstitious is countered by broadcasting programmes. Local songs and popular talks with local colour are interspersed with small doses of instruction. In Hyderabad broadcasting initiated in Urdu and in English is to be expanded with programmes in Tamil, Telugu, and Kanarese.

A colossal expansion of the power of this tool will be open to the Government of India when it has the courage to let the great voices of India like Gandhi and Nehru speak in ways parallel to those practised in Britain when, for instance, a general election is imminent or some issue of great moment is in the arena of national discussion.

The journalism of India lies at the heart of its future, for it is bound to exercise a powerful influence on the spirit that will prevail in the political and social life of the crucial period ahead of us. It may sting the Indian and European into even more and more exacerbated antagonisms or lead them to discover a way of co-operation. While unable myself to read the vernacular papers—and indeed there are few Indians who can read those of provinces beyond their own language area —I found real illumination in reading the Indian newspapers printed in English, such as the *Amrita Bazar Patrika* of Calcutta. While often acid in their criticism of British rule, the presentation of news by the

Indian papers is generally fairly balanced. Among them *The Hindu* of Madras by common consent stands head and shoulders above the rest. Indeed, to my mind there is in the country no more readable, informative newspaper, Indian or European, than *The Hindu*, one of whose notable features is its sustained survey of the new books of the West as well as of the East. The happy experience of ten days' continuous work in Mysore with the provincial representatives of newspapers from all over India, handling news matter that had dynamite in it if unscrupulously exploited, revealed a body of young Indians, alert, sympathetic, frank, and humorous, with a keen eye for news-interest combined with a scrupulous care in handling it. I do not expect to find anywhere in the world a body of men worthier to sustain the best traditions of journalism than these anonymous servants of the public with whom I worked in an Indian State. No memory of the months in India gives me livelier pleasure than this comradeship, which came to its climax in what they humorously called a 'dry and modest banquet' to which the Mysore Association of Journalists entertained me at the close of our work together.

On the European side of journalism in India, interviews with Mr. Francis Low of *The Times of India* in Bombay, Mr. Hailes of the *Madras Mail*, Mr. Wordsworth of *The Statesman* at Calcutta and Mr. Alexander Inglis of *The Times* of London at Delhi, as well as those holding the responsible position exercised by Reuters as a channel of news with the whole world, showed me that, while their attitude to Indian politics varies as their gifts are varied, a balanced realistic view prevails that is unready to lend itself to any harsh or extremist policies.

The dangerous inflammatory element in Indian journalism lies in the multitude of little local 'rags', generally cheaply produced by one man in a country town. These spread among the village people fantastic lies and garbled reports. The village readers of these papers, and the far wider group of those who listen to their reading, have no knowledge by which to correct the false vilifications that then pass from mouth to mouth among the peasant population. This is one of the many factors that should lead the Government of India to take broadcasting as seriously and adventurously as some of the Indian States like Mysore and Hyderabad are doing. It is a long, difficult task, including technical problems like the development of the project of communal village receiving sets and a battery service on a wide scale; but broadcasting is the only way in which Indian and British leaders can speak direct to illiterate India in city and village.

Talks on the boat with a prominent Sikh merchant of Lahore gave me the first of numerous contacts with that powerful but normally silent force in India, the men whose hands hold the threads of international commerce. The burly, turbaned, grey-bearded form of Sardar Sahib Supuran Singh Chawla of Lahore is familiar to the merchants in Prague, purchasing Czechoslovakian wares for Indian households, in Berlin negotiating for steel-rails, in Stockholm, London, Paris, and Rome. He has his business relationships, indeed, in every capital in Europe save Moscow. In India his other business interests run from the control of cinemas to interest in tanneries. Men of like breadth of commercial contact I met in the comradeship of the Rotary Clubs of Lahore, Calcutta, Madras, and Bombay. In any attempt to assess the India of to-day, we cannot even grasp what is happening to the village life of India without watching the activities of these men. Through their ledgers run the accounts and on their way-bills are recorded transport to India of the ship-loads of European, Japanese, or American-made hoes, hurricane lamps, enamelled bowls, cotton-prints, sandals, ploughshares, tins of petrol, motor-bus chassis, the cinema films and machines that now penetrate the life of the villages of India. Those goods, as we have seen, are transforming the very structure of village India. They put out of work the smith, the weaver, and other hand-craftsmen. They thus destroy the old *jajmani* system that made the village an economically secure self-contained unit riveted together by the exchange not of money but of services. They withdraw from the village in payment for goods wealth that used to remain within its mud-walls. They incarnate that advance into India of western and far eastern mechanized civilization in which Gandhi has seen a 'Satanic' attack on the very soul of India; a civilization, however, which is as irresistible as the tides and through which it would seem inevitable that the world must pass. Indeed, from one aspect the great gulf between the policy of Gandhi and that of Nehru is that the former would hold back that onrush, while the other would pass through it to the collective mastery and control of mechanism for the service of man that lies at the heart of his socialist policy. Meanwhile, however, the merchant holds the field.

I talked with a well-known Indian doctor, with a finely sensitive face, who spoke affectionately of Cambridge and of his undergraduate days. Delicate in perception, acute in argument, cultured, humorous, he was a delightful companion. Born a Hindu, he had no use for institutional religion. 'I would not say that I do not believe there is a God,' he said, somewhat wistfully, 'but I'm afraid I don't believe that God cares very much about us or about what goes on here.' A convinced nationalist, he could see little good for India in the British connexion.

'Do you see no hope then in the new constitution?' I asked.

'No,' he said definitely, 'I think we should have nothing to do with it. It gives us nothing more in reality. All those safeguards . . . 85 per cent of the revenue will still be under British control, and there are so many regulations about the other 15 per cent that in reality we can always be prevented from spending it in the way we want.'

'But,' I said, 'if every one followed you in this it would mean that all the best men, those who care most for India, would stand aside and leave place-hunters in power. Don't you think that a man like you ought to try to work from within the governmental framework instead of standing aside?'

Sadly he shook his head. 'No, I couldn't do that. . . .'

Speaking about the doctor later with an English friend who knew him well, I learned that he was as able a politician as he was a doctor—a persuasive, eloquent speaker, who could go far in the political sphere. But because he had no sympathy with the alien government which ruled his country he felt unable to put his gifts at her disposal. There are thousands of men like him in India at the present time.

With a sense of shock we learned from our mutual

friend that the doctor's wife was in purdah, was indeed illiterate. What a pity that he hadn't an educated wife to be his companion! Our friend smiled. 'Don't waste too much of your pity,' he remarked. 'In many cases, of course, these men are married when they are young and have no choice. But even if they had, many of them would still choose an uneducated wife, a woman mentally inferior. You see, a man like the doctor, who appears to you so western in his ideas, has other sides. Our western culture does not really go down to the roots of his being. It is a slab superimposed on older traditional ways of thought. We have westernized his mind, but not the emotional springs of his action. You can't change the deep emotional reactions of a race in one generation or in two or three. . . . A good part of the malaise of Indian life comes from this.'

I thought of all the many Indians I had met. . . .

'This superimposition of western mental discipline on youth whose emotional springs of life have been developed in the company of an illiterate Indian mother really means then that very few of those who have received a western education are what the psychologist would call unified personalities? They live in layers, as it were, and the layers have never properly come to terms with each other.'

'Yes, that is the trouble.'

'It is difficult,' I commented, 'to see how things are to get better. Take the doctor's children, for instance. They will be given a western education, no doubt. But in their most impressionable years their emotional attitudes are being formed by an uneducated mother and grandmother steeped in the old superstitions and at variance with so much that will later appear to their intellect as desirable. Yet all their lives they will feel the undertow of emotions beyond the control of their reason, and will not even recognize where the root of the trouble lies.'

'But the western education we give is largely to blame, too,' said our friend. He is a professor in an old-established Christian college, and sees India's problems, probably rightly, largely in terms of education. 'We shall never get any further until we educate the emotions as we have tried to educate the mind. Modern civilization seems to me about to commit suicide because we have suppressed emotional releases. In education we are tied down to cramming our students to pass exams in English.' He said that the best men were conscious of the hollowness of it all. He saw them bound hand and foot with red tape and sacrificed to the Moloch of a top-heavy system, and many of them leave educational work in India for a sphere which gives more scope for putting their ideals into practice. He felt that progress was impossible until the present educational system in India was smashed. In its place he would try to build a system of elementary education designed to train the emotions as well as the mind—'education for life', as Booker Washington said of the education of ex-slaves in the southern states of North America. Education of older students should be more largely on technical lines, training them in the skills that India needs if she is to become healthy, well-fed, and economically self-supporting.

I thought of the children I had seen at Moga, where Dr. and Mrs. Harper, following Dr. McKee, have developed a scheme of elementary education which might well be an example to all India. Indeed, Government is now looking to Dr. and Mrs. Harper and their very able headmaster, the Christian son of a Hindu fakir, for help; and they are giving short intensive courses of training to village teachers in their development of the project method, and even more in the ideals of which that is the expression. Through the 'project' method of education, the child is given both an incentive to learn and a joyous freedom of disciplined self-expression.

It was a novel experience to walk into a classroom of children all so busily absorbed that they did not notice my entry and then to discover after a few minutes of watching that there was no teacher with them. I found that they were deep in a project which had been begun weeks before. They were planning a garden, and that had grown by the children's own eager inventive interest into inquiries about all kinds of vegetables and trees, then to an imaginary gardener and his family, the house they were to live in, their clothing and furniture and even pictures. They had built the little house, which involved arithmetic, mensuration, weights and measures, and other subjects. When I entered the room the boys were at work planning and creating the furniture and the girls the clothes that the doll-gardener, his wife, and children were to wear. In this same connexion they had just given a wedding party for the gardener's family to which the teaching staff of Moga were invited, and were startled during the meal to get short addresses from the children on the values of the foods, manners at table, the necessity to chew and not gobble, and other valuable education for life.

The whole life of the school is run on the lines of small group families. It was fascinating to watch the eager intentness with which two boys made the fire in the outdoor oven, mixed the dough, rolled the paste, and proceeded to bake the *chapaties* for all the fellows in their own little home.

The result of education given on these lines over a sufficient number of years leads to the production of balanced, integrated personalities, rooted in the soil of India yet open to the winds of all the world, who do not divorce reason from emotion or thought from action, but who see life steadily and see it whole. Has India any greater need to-day than the creation of such personalities?

. . . .

We are watching, as it were, a drama on a stupendous stage without being able to see to what climax either of tragedy or happiness it may lead. To the Indian of all types and classes the villain of the piece is the British Government. To the more detached onlooker, however intense may be his sympathy with Indian aspirations toward unity and freedom, a host of other gigantic and evil forces looms up—dirt, disease, illiteracy, grinding poverty, exploitation. From these spring lethargy, terrible anaemia, paralysis of will, fatalism. Without trying to pronounce judgement on Mr. Edwyn Bevan's thesis that India is not weak because she is a subject people but subject because she is weak, one may well hold that she should not wait until the British Government has disappeared before endeavouring to slay these giants that hold her in thraldom.

INDEX

Agricultural Colony, ex-*détenu*, 87–8.
Ahmadiya sect, 116.
Ahmed, Khan Bahadur Syed, 154.
Aiyer, Sir C. P. Ramaswami, 131.
Ajanta caves, 153–62.
Akbar, 110.
Allegory of Love, The, 14, 34.
Amrita Bazar Patrika, 181.
Anderson, Sir John, 77, 78, 80, 81, 82, 87, 115.
Anglo-Indian community, 176–7.
Armstrong, Miss, 69.
Art and Meditation, 74.
Art, Indian, 53–4, 155–62.
Aziz, Mr., 21–3.

Bahrita, 51.
Bangalore Silk and Woollen Mills, 147.
Barker, Ernest, 3, 39, 70.
Benares, *see* Chapter VI.
Bengal, partition of, 79.
— terrorism in, 54.
Bengali drama, 57–8.
— literature, 52–3, 56–9.
Bevan, Edwyn, 189.
Bombay chawls, 98–102.
Bose, Sarat, 77.
Bose, Subash Chandra, 176.
Brabourne, Lord, 104, 115, 179.
Brayne, F. L., 33.
Britain and India, 46–9, 83, 91–7, 104, 174.
Broadcasting, 33, 179–81, 183.
Buddhism, 72–4, 155–6.

Caird, Dr. Edward, 105.
Calcutta University, 78–9.
Cauvery River dam, 147.
Chakravarty, A. C., 52.
Chawlà, Sardar Sahib Supuran Singh, 183.
Chirol, Sir Valentine, 3.
Christianity, 65, 69, 73, 115, 130–2.
Cinemas, 12, 16, 59–60.
Commercial Museum, Calcutta, 81–3.
Communal Award, 172–3.
Communalism, 44, 92, 172–3.
Congress, 105, 113, 114, 176.
— meeting, 84.
— Socialist Party, 44, 103.
Constitution, new Indian, 28–9, 113, 152, 177, 185.
Culture of Women, The, 18.
Curzon, Lord, 79, 80, 94.

Das, R. C., 65–6.
Datta, S. K., 3.
Day, The, 72.
Delhi, 111, 118.
Depressed classes, 126–7, 130–2, 135.
Desai, Mahadeo, 123.
Détenus, 77, 78–83, 87–9.
Doms, 66–70.
Dornakal, Bishop of, 130–1.
Duff, Alexander, 78.
Dutt, Dr., 57, 58.

Education, 55, 69, 78, 148–50, 187–9.
Electricity, 147, 179.
Elmhurst, Mr. and Mrs., 132–3.
Erode, 12, 163.

Fakirs, 63.
Famine, 47.
Farquhar, J. N., 3.
Fatepur Sikri, 110–11.
Feroze-ud-Din, Miss, 16–17.
Fielden, Lionel, 33, 179–80.
Films, Indian, 59–60, 127–30.

Gandhi, M. K., 11, 23, 36, 38, 42–3, 45–6, 53, 79, 85–6, 92, 106, 122–3, 126–7, 130, 131, 136–7, 138–40, 146, 163, 169, 181, 184.

Gandhi, Mrs., 125–6.
Gate of Victory, 110–11.
Ghose, G. D., 133.
Glimpses of World History, 49.
Gourijore, 87.
Govinda, Anagarika, 73–4.
Gupta, Shiva Prasad, 72.

Hailes, Mr., 182.
Halifax, Lord, 35.
Hamilton, Sir Daniel, 33.
Haque, Hon. Khan Bahadur M. Azizal, 77.
Harijan, 123.
Harper, Dr. and Mrs., 187–8.
Hatch, K., 33.
Higginbottom, Sam, 27, 28, 29, 30, 31.
Hindu, The, 182.
Hindu University, 70.
Hinduism, 64, 65, 71–2, 75–6, 107, 115.
Hindustan Times, 176.
Hydari, Sir Akbar, 148, 152, 153–4.
Hyderabad, 148–51, 153–4, 181.
—, Nizam of, 148.
— State Women's Conference, 169.

Id, Feast of, 17, 110, 117, 118–21.
Indian Listener, 180.
Indian States, 147–8, 152.
Indian Struggle, The, 176.
Industrial Centre, ex-*détenu*, 88–9.
Inglis, Alexander, 182.
International Fellowship, 77.
Iqbal, Sir Mohammed, 21, 22, 23–6, 50, 56.
Irrigation, 47, 147.
Islam, 64, 116, 118–21.
Ismail, Sir Mirza, 142–5.
Itarsi, 5.

Jackson, J. C., 66.
Jajmani, 184.
Jayaker, M. R., 105.
Journalism, Indian, 181–3.
Justice Party, 164.

Kali festival, 75–6.
Karma, 30, 178.
Kemal Ataturk, 25.
Khan, Khan Abdul Gaffar, 123–5.
Khan, Sir Muhammad Zafrullah, 116–18.
Khudai Khidmatgar, 123.

Lahore, 19–21, 170.
Legislative Assembly, 112, 114–15.
Linlithgow, Lord, 28, 33, 112, 115.
Literature, Indian, *see* Chapter V.
Lothian, Lord, 39.
Low, Francis, 182.
Lowenfeld, Dr. Madge, 55.

MacDonald, Ramsay, 172.
Mackenzie, Dr. and Mrs., 102–3.
Macmurray, John, 55.
Madras Mail, 182.
Mahadevan, P., 43.
Marriage, 15–16.
Martandum, 33.
Maslandpur, 87.
Mattai, Dr. John, 112, 115, 134.
McKee, Dr., 187.
Mitter, B. L., 86–7, 115.
Moga, 187–9.
Morris, William, 163.
Mother India, Temple to, 71–2.
Motor-bus, effect of, 11–12.
Music, Indian, 51.
Mysore, 142–5, 147, 148, 178–9, 180–1.
— Association of Journalists, 182.
—, Maharaja of, 146.

Nag, Dr. Kalidas, 60.
Naidu, Sarojini, 61.
Naikkar, E. V. Ramaswami, 163–5.
Nasik, 179.
Nawaz, Begum Shah, 13–14.
Nehru, Jawaharlal, 35–46, 49, 53, 61, 85, 86, 95, 96, 139, 146, 152, 168–9, 175, 177–8, 181, 184.
Newspapers, 106.
Nietzsche, 22–3, 24–5.
Nyogi, Mr., 81–3.

Osmania University, 148–9, 170.

Pandit, Mr. and Mrs. Ranjit Sitaram, 36.
Parachiya group, 56–9, 77.
Paul, K. T., 3.
P.E.N. Club, 60–1.
Phoenix Club, 94.
Pilgrims, Hindu, 62–3, 75.
Police, 79–81, 88.
Population, 70, 86, 116.
Purdah, 16, 17, 118, 150–2, 186.

Qadir, Sir Abdul, 13.

Railway travel, 5–11.
Ram Krishna mission, 134.
Ramazan, Fast of, 16–17, 116.
Recovery Plan for Bengal, 87.
'Red Shirts', 123–5.
Report of the Commission on Unemployment, 39.
Revolt, 163.
Rise and Fulfilment of British Rule in India, The, 79.
Rotary Clubs, 183–4.
Roy, Dr. B. C., 38, 77, 84–6.
Royal Commission on Agriculture, 33, 39.
Rural reconstruction, 28–9, 33, 53, 54, 127–30, 133–5.

St. Paul's College, 77.
Salt-march, 138–9.
Santiniketan, 53–5.
Sapru, Sir Tej Bahadur, 39–40.
Saranath, 72–4.
Scottish Churches' College, 77–8.
Secret of the Self, The, 25.
Segaon, 122, 125, 126.
Self-Respect Movement, 164.
Serampore College, 77.
Servants of India, 134.
Shehvar, Princess Durru, 169.
Smuts, General, 95.
Socialism, 40.
Solomon, Captain Gladstone, 154, 160.
Spencer, Miss, 68.
Spooner, Professor, 25.
Sriniketan, 133.
Statesman, The, 75, 182.
Stephens, Ian, 116.
Sukchur, 87.

Tagore, Rabindranath, 33, 44–5, 50, 52–3, 54, 56, 77, 132–3.
Taj Mahal, 109–10.
Taj, S. Nitiaz Ali, 18.
Tamil literature, 50–2.
Temple entry, 106, 132.
Terrorism, 54, 78–83.
Thompson, Edward, 79.
Times of India, The, 182.
Times, The, 182.
Transmigration, doctrine of, 27–8.
Travancore, 131.
—, Maharaja of, 131.

United Services Club, Calcutta, 75, 76.

Van Moody, Mrs. William John, 132.
Village Improvement Movement, 179.

Wadia, Madam Sophia, 60.
Wadia, Professor A. S., 56, 135–6, 149.
Wardha, 122.
Widows, 63–4.
Wigram, Dr., 124.
Women, emancipation of, 106, 150–2, 169–71.
Wordsworth, Mr., 75, 76–7, 182.

Y.M.C.A., 33, 146.
Yoga, 164–5.